M4C 5L6

BRIGHTER RED

AN IMMIGRANT SON ENVISIONS CANADA

KEVIN LOBO

TUNDRA WOLF
PUBLICATIONS

Copyright © 2010 by Kevin J Lobo
All Rights Reserved

No part of this book may be reproduced stored in a retrieval system, or transmitted in any form by any means, graphic, electronic, or mechanical, photocopying, recording or otherwise, or by any information storage, without the prior written permission of the publishers.

Library and Archives Canada Cataloguing in Publication

Lobo, Kevin, 1966-
Brighter red : an immigrant son envisions Canada / Kevin Lobo.

Includes bibliographical references and index.
Issued also in electronic format.

ISBN 978-0-9865053-24

1. Social problems—Canada. 2. Canada—Social conditions. 3. Canada—Politics and government—21st century. 4. Lobo, Kevin, 1966-. 5. Immigrants—Cultural assimilation—Canada. I. Title.

HN103.5.L63 2010   301.0971   C2010-900627-5

References to websites in this book are current as of the publication date. These references may not be available at a future date due to the nature of internet content.

The publisher has made every effort to provide/cite and obtain permission for material referenced to in this book. Any omissions noticed can be brought to the attention of the publisher and will be corrected in subsequent editions.

TUNDRA WOLF PUBLICATIONS
5 LANARK AVENUE
TORONTO, ONTARIO M6C 2B2

Publisher: Tundra Wolf Publications – www.tundrawolfpublications.com
kevinlobo@tundrawolfpublications.com
Editor: Alex Coelho
Cover/Title/Book Design: Gavin Barrett
Printed by: Lightning Source International
Printed in: USA

Acknowledgements

From a simple realization of a new home country to a passion to do something about it, this book is the culmination of many personal experiences. However, for someone with no publishing experience to transalate those pages, notes and scribbles into a book is the reflection of the tremendous help I have received along the way.

My greatest thanks, goes to Gavin Barrett. The same Gavin who picked me up from the airport on arrival for the first time in Canada. For his help, guidance, critical comments and encouragement in helping this book along the way, I am truly grateful. The artwork, the design, the cover and the very title, I owe it to Gavin.

To Maria Watts, a quiet voice, a deep soul and a true friend. The first person on this planet who I had the confidence to walk up to talk about my book and who in return, showered me with barrels of wisdom from every Canadian and spiritual angle.

To Lynn, my friend, soulmate, wife and critic. Her, "you go boy", steely strong encouragement, and her A+++ after reading my initial writings encouraged me to have confidence in myself and pursue this dream.

DEDICATION

To,

Mabel,

my mummy,

whose tremendous life

of sacrifice and courage

helped me reach this day and

whose amazing courage

still inspires me.

Rest in Peace.

How to read this book?
From the Author's perspective, here are some tips about the structure of this book.

Born into Canada

The first five chapters are an account of my journey to Canada, the golden dawn of any new immigrant's dream. The prologue and chapters 1 to 4 are my first years in Canada, from forming my Canadian identity, adopting my new home, growing into it and then on to embracing it whole heartedly. It is a love affair that attracts any new immigrant; to love their new home but to also get in touch with the realities of life in Canada.

'**O Canada**', **The 'Canada' Dream, Coming to Canada** and **A Canadian Conscience** are these chapters of discovery.

Some Ugly Canadian Issues

As in life, every Canadian is faced with issues that reflect the eternal struggle, the good and the bad. Whether one acknowledges them or not, they affect us, every single one of us Canadians, directly and indirectly.

Do you care about these issues or are you in tune with them to know that many Canadians suffer due to these social injustices. Chapters 5 to 11 delve into issues like **poverty, child poverty, First Nations, education, crime, sports** and our sense of achievement and the hot issue of **global warming**. Each of these issues affects us deeply and these chapters aim to invite you, fellow Canadians, to give it a thought.

A New Canada

This section filled with personal anecdotes is my dream of what Canada should be and where we should be headed. As in any democracy, Politicians take centre stage in moving the country ahead, whether it is new laws, taxes, green technologies or a myriad of other issues. So do they really serve us as we would expect them to? How do you perceive the future? Can we think anew and create a new Canada, one that moves from being good to being the best.

Chapters 12 to 17, invite us to look ahead and create a brand new society. One built upon the current good. '**The Great Political Divide**' and '*That* **Government in Ottawa**' look for renewed connections between us, our politicians and the issues that matter. '**A Higher Calling**', '**My Canada**' and '**Brighter Red: A New Tomorrow**' are the author's invitation to you to look through a new lens into a new Canada, one that cares for all Canadians and looks to definitively move beyond the current ills that afflict us.

Table of Contents

SECTION 1: Born into Canada

Prologue	Prologue	11
Chapter 1	O 'Canada'	17
Chapter 2	The 'Canada' Dream	25
Chapter 3	Coming to Canada	33
Chapter 4	A Canadian Conscience	39

SECTION 2: Some Ugly Canadian Issues

Chapter 5	The Shameful Reality: Poverty	49
Chapter 6	The Unending Tragedy: Child Poverty	63
Chapter 7	Canada's Own Third World Nation	75
Chapter 8	A University Education for All	91
Chapter 9	Youth and Crime	111
Chapter 10	Fat Kids or Gold Medallists	123
Chapter 11	To Green Gold	139

SECTION 3: A New Canada

Chapter 12	Politically Correct or Incorrect	155
Chapter 13	The Great Political Divide	167
Chapter 14	*That* Government in Ottawa	181
Chapter 15	A Higher Calling	195
Chapter 16	My Canada	207
Chapter 17	Brighter Red: A New Tomorrow	221
References		227
INDEX		229

Born into Canada

Prologue

Prologue

It had been a long 11-hour flight

across the Pacific Ocean. Starting from Hong Kong and now descending into Alaska for a refuelling stop; I craned over my sleeping neighbour to catch a view through the partially open window. It was the second-last leg of my long journey into a new land that was soon to be my home, Canada. My memory raced back to the years gone by, when leaving India for the first time and heading to the Middle East. Then, as that flight descended, my eyes had caught sight of the endless desert. It had seemed lifeless and barren, matching the fears in my heart as I headed into that first job abroad. Six years later, this was Alaska and we were almost ready for touchdown when a huge mop of green caught my eye. Even in that fleeting instant those forests looked majestic. The fatigue and sleepless daze vanished in an instant and I did not need any prodding from the stewardess for a mandatory evacuation to allow for a cleanup of the aircraft.

The wood panelled airport seemed homely, almost rural, as I raced to a giant glass window. The view was breathtaking. The mountains in the distance and the endlessly stretching green forest seemed to seamlessly begin where the runway left off into a perfect curve. The vision of that majestic view seemed welcomingly interrupted as a giant 747 made a flawless touchdown. Nature and technology seemed so beautifully married at that point, unlike the shanty-towns of Mumbai that I had become so used to. "Beautiful", I gasped, turning and hoping to catch somebody next to me to share the moment. I recoiled in fright, but the scare lasted for a moment as I realized the giant figure sharing that view with me was a stuffed grizzly bear, standing upright and looking menacing even in death. Thankfully, a giggle brought my attention to the other side. Another sleepy head like me, "Don't worry, he won't bite", he said. "Still beautiful", I said trying to change the subject to the original object of my beauty. He agreed wholeheartedly. He had grown up in a similar mountainous region, "Not here, but in Canada" he told me. A quick introduction and the giggly figure was all fatherly as I explained to him that it was my first time heading into Canada. I imagined him feeling like a pro, an expert, or the grand old native lecturing the novice.

"You're heading into one of the most beautiful countries, with the most wonderful people in the world", he told me. In that little conversation, I peppered him with questions of every kind. He was after all the first Canadian I was speaking to. A beautiful specimen of a beautiful land, I heard my mind say and label and catalogue the memory of that moment.

The journey to Canada had been almost half way around the world, starting in Oman, stops in three cities in India, through Bangkok, to a few days in Singapore with my sister, and finally all the way around the eastern half of the globe, from Hong Kong to this moment in Anchorage, Alaska. There was still the final eight-hour leg to cover, the final flight to Toronto. The announcements reminded us of that, as he sought to say bye and catch a bit of the break before the final flight. "One final question", I begged him. "I hope you don't mind", I heard myself saying apologetically, my tone changing to soften him up for the last one. "Okay, shoot", he said. I couldn't look him in the eye for this one. I chose instead to

PROLOGUE

look down at our Cathay Pacific Airbus A340 parked just below us. My mind seemed to equate that question with that aircraft, the final conduit into what lay ahead.

"Will I face discrimination of any kind, color, race, or origin, anything that a newcomer needs to know?" He gazed thoughtfully, the initial retort that may have cropped in his mind betrayed by the rush of blood to his face, now given to meaningful thought. He probably sensed that his response would define my experience and perception of Canada for many years to come. "Ask yourself this question a few years into your life in Canada", he told me thoughtfully. A long pause with a deep look, as I now looked into his face. "Your whole life and experience will innately tell you at some stage that even if you were never born here, you always belonged".

O 'Canada' 17

O 'Canada'

Canada, O Canada, our beautiful

country, our rich country, loved and cherished, treasured and longed for, unoccupied and free! That is the Canada we love; that is the Canada we live in. A Canada that attracts, not repels, a Canada that gives, not receives, a Canada that provides. That is why ours is a country that attracts admiration, even envy. That is why ours is a country of dreams, a destination where humanity can be found.

This book is my short journey of discovering that Canada, the one so good and obvious, the nice Canada that everyone knows. It is also about my discovery of another Canada…one that is hidden beneath the good, one that is not so pleasant and beautiful. Thank you for joining me on this journey. It's a story, based on life, on Canada and Canadians. It's a story and a view, a dream and a vision, about a journey that millions of Canadians have made, the ones that immigrated here, as well as those that were born here. For those blessed and fortunate to be born in this country and those who have made it their home, it is nothing short of a blessing. A country blessed with liberty, respect, wealth, natural resources, beauty, and almost every good thing that one could dream about in a nation.

For the millions of immigrants who have arrived here over the decades, with dreams and hopes, and the desire to live a better life, it's a dream that, by default, is always realized for most immigrants, thanks to a nation that provides for all. It's a dream that succeeds for some in small measure and for many in large measures. It's a dream that turns to reality, a reality that encompasses the basics of life that are always provided. The one time in life where the good dream always comes true. The greatest of these is the liberty to think, to be, to be realized, to be known, to be accepted, and to prosper.

How do you find your Canadian identity? When do you feel Canadian? What are those moments when your heart stops, or bumps along faster, you feel the surge of emotion, the little tear in your eye, and lots of pride? When are the moments when the sight of the beautiful *Maple Leaf*, fluttering with glory, gives you that proud sense of being Canadian? Is it at the Olympics when you see our athletes on the victory stand or, at other the end of the spectrum, as you stand on the *Highway of Heroes*? As you wait with sadness and with pride to salute our brave men and women passing by on their last journey? Those brave solders having paid that ultimate price for the safety of the world? Is anger an emotion that you ever feel, knowing your country has been harmed? In words, in deeds, in actions, in ridicule, or even in humor, do you ever feel wronged as a Canadian, internationally? Do you ever feel the insult to the Canadian pride that tells you it was wrong? Does it make you want to fight back, retaliate, or simply state the truth and feel justice has been served, something I think most Canadians would do?

Is fanatical patriotism a part of our daily bread? Hardly so. Negative as that may sound, it reflects a sense of stability and prosperity that we enjoy. How often do you have to stand up to the world and defend Canada? What do you do on *Canada Day*? Hoist the national flag, sing *O Canada*, organize your own event, your own song, bake some treats richly decorated in red and white, and then enjoy the fireworks? Yet, challenged or not, our Canadian identity is more about the niceness of life. It is not about a hard-fought freedom struggle, or about liberation from a foreign rule. It is not about hundreds of lives laid down to win the freedom of this country; rather, hundreds of lives laid down, contributed for the safety of the world. It's about the beauty of life, a beautiful country, a beautiful life, material riches, and the peaceful feeling that insecurity about tomorrow hardly ever crosses the blue skies ahead. It's a story about collaboration, cooperation, and confederation.

To all of us, who live and enjoy of this bounty, comes a responsibility as well. To preserve it, cherish it, enrich it, and then pass it on to the next generation of Canadians. It is like a journey that could be so easily forgotten amid the comforts of life. It is a responsibility that can be so easily shirked, knowing that we could drift to tomorrow, and the day after, without worrying. Yet, amid the comforts of life, it becomes a responsibility to pay attention to all that is not well, to all who do not have, and to all that needs to be fixed. The call to public service may be for the few who undertake it, for the best of reasons; but for the rest it is a journey that has to be lived.

How do you perceive your country? It's a question rarely asked, yet so implicit to our being in this age of international closeness. The US, Europe, Africa, and the East are not too far. The internet and information technology revolution have made sure we are connected like never before. Yet, how much are we connected with our inner *national self*?

One of my most interesting experiences, when new in Canada in 1999, was asking Canadians about the *parental gender* of the country. Yes, you read that right, the *gender*. In India, the nation is a mother, and scores of patriotic poems, songs, and even movies, are dedicated to the *Motherland*. The country is referred to, literally, as *Mother India* or, in

Hindi, *Bharat Mata*. In Germany, it is the *Fatherland*. So, I would ask people, genuinely, at first, is it the *motherland* or the *fatherland*? People would look right through me, or get back to their chores, with a smirk, wondering if I hadn't anything better to do. Do you love the *motherland* or the *fatherland*? "What nation are you referring to?" they would ask back. (I'm not sure if I left them with a thought about what it really is or here was someone with some strange things to ask.) No one was sure. Do you run into a flood of movies, produced in Canada, that have the good patriotic guys, the Canadian heroes, fighting the bad guys, whoever they maybe? Even, hypothetically, it would be rare to imagine that. How about *Aliens*? Would they be interested? The US has scores of them like that. The *Men in Black*. What would our version of that be? Simply said, it means we don't see our freedom challenged. And so, from someone who has heard freedom struggles stories firsthand, who felt the anger of having been occupied, even after being granted freedom, this is a little tale of what I would like Canadians to feel.

Starting out on our immigration dream, as we looked to that beautiful land, a *foreign country*, as we called it, as we had seen it in movies, we dreamed of that new land of milk and honey, of equality and justice, of riches and opportunities. Despite the information available, and as I am sure simple common sense would explain better, you turn a blind eye to the bad and look at the good. And so, for immigrants like me, Canada beckoned as the Promised Land, the Perfect Land! And so, while we celebrate the riches and the plenty, let's look at the lack of it as well. As we celebrate the goodness of life, let's look at the lack of it. As we celebrate success, let's take a look at the failures. As we celebrate justice and equality, let's take a very long look at injustice and inequality, as well. Let's put them both in perspective, without demeaning the *haves*, let's bring the *have-nots* into the picture. For, it is the *haves* that allow us to feel good and do it for the *have-nots,* too. This is my journey of discovery through nine insightful years, nine years of simple success and achievement, nine years of living a beautiful life, and nine years that inspire me to look back and give back, give back to society and to those in that society that have not gotten the fruit that has blossomed so abundantly. This is not about laws, regulations, statutes, numbers, statistics or policies, nor will you find a column called *management.* This is my raw emotional account — from one Canadian to another.

The 'Canada' Dream 25

The 'Canada' Dream

My journey to Canada began in the

hot sands of the Middle East in a country called the Sultanate of Oman. There, hundreds of thousands of expatriates, or *expats* as we were referred to, came to work, earn some extra money, save for the future and return home successful—financially. They filled every rung of the ladder, from the bottom to the very top.

In most Middle East countries, rich in oil and loaded with so-called petro-dollars but woefully short of labor, there was a need for workers of every kind, trained and untrained — executives with fancy MBAs, as well as street sweepers and washroom cleaners. Others advised their royal highnesses or made critical investment decisions and ran the banks and the ministries. There were jobs aplenty.

In that sun-drenched land, work was the only religion. On arrival, you submitted your passport to your employer or sponsor, who controlled your life, your driving license, your work permit, your liquor permit, your visa, and your travel arrangements. Yes, it was a kind of bondage, with pay, perks, pampered living, paid vacation days and, of course, no taxes. You loved it, at first, when your flight landed amidst those endless vistas of sun-bathed deserts, modern highways and modern cities.

You settled into your fancy accommodation — a fancy villa

with a Mercedes, perhaps, — if you were high enough on the corporate ladder. If you were at the bottom, working at a construction site in 49-50 degrees Celsius, you got used to sharing a dorm and a single washroom with several others and a beat-up old air conditioner chugging away fruitlessly. As you waited for your first pay cheque, you picked up the dos and don'ts of the place.

Life was tough and hard, but financially very rewarding. You had money to spend. You lived comfortably. You could drive a fancy car, and save and send money to your folks back home. You worked early morning to late evening, with a Thursday-Friday weekend.

It was an Islamic country, of course, so Friday was the official Sunday. You went from week to week, workday to workday, waiting and counting the days till the odd holiday came along, generally coupled with a weekend, to give you a break. You had some fun, depending on your circle of friends and your ability to socialize, within the permitted limits.

If you've never been there, hopefully, this helps you picture what life was like. If you've been there and lived and worked there, you know that these few paragraphs barely touch the surface of that experience.

In short, no matter how much money you made or how high or low on the ladder you were, you were always a second-class citizen. Your sponsor got you the job. If you were not needed, or found wanting, you could be packed off, no explanations given, in just a few hours. You may have been planning your evening workout at the local Intercontinental one minute, the next you could be before the personnel manager signing your termination letter and settlement and then dropped off at the airport where someone would have dumped all your belongings, having packed them all for you. And then you were gone.

It was a quasi-satisfying life, dependent on your dreams and expectations. By the end of the first year, definitely, you would be in some kind of a depression longing for your first vacation, fully paid with airfare and all.

The very depressing day you returned from vacation, you'd swear that the next vacation home would be on a one-way ticket and you would save every penny so that you would have enough to buy or build your first home, or pay off a mortgage or comfortably educate your kids.

For most that would never happen. The very few daring and ambitious ones broke away early. Others got stuck there for years or for the better years of their lives. There were some who knew that after years of pampered living, going home was not an option. Those who came from less privileged countries like India loved the luxury, but hated the bondage. So, naturally, they thought of "a better life" elsewhere.

As for me, I was an IT guy, somewhere on the middle rungs of the corporate ladder. I earned a comfortable salary, with enough perks, a house with all the necessary utilities, a car, as well as a paid vacation with the taxi fare to the airport thrown in.

I had many young friends to spend my evenings and weekends with. I could party and picnic every weekend, catch a bit of sports and generally complain for the sake of complaining.

It was a privileged kind of life, in a sense. I, like a lot of other young professionals, was a source of pride back home. I splurged on fancy electronics but still managed to send enough to my parents. They didn't need it, they simply saved it up for me, in case I landed back home, broke and kicked out of a job.

So where does Canada come into all this? The dream of "a

better life" — that's what Canada was. The Middle East was rife with immigration lawyers and agencies. Immigration to Australia, Canada or New Zealand was the way to go, in that order. For IT guys, there was always the H-1B visa route to the US. Many made it that way, dreaming of having a green card some day or maybe, eventually, US citizenship.

My love affair with Canada began oddly with *The X-files*, the TV series with FBI agents Fox Mulder and Dana Sculley chasing paranormal entities, scientific freaks, incarnated spirits saving traditional sacred lands, aliens, ghosts and of course, 'the Government' that hid everything from its citizens. The show that became a religion to millions of science fiction and paranormal-loving and alien-curious fans became my passion too. The outdoor locations where the series was shot had beautiful blue lakes bordered by thick forests, beautiful cities, and serene, unending countrysides. Somewhere along the way I discovered that it was all shot in Canada. Cupid's arrow had struck home. That's where I wanted to be. From then on everything I did revolved around that goal.

I confess that my knowledge of Canada was limited, then. I'd heard of Montreal, thanks to the Olympics. And, even though my school-learned general knowledge was pretty good, I struggled to place Ottawa.

Fr. Lester, my parish priest in Muscat, capital of Oman, once spoke of beautiful British Columbia. To hide my ignorance I kept my mouth shut. Luckily so, because a search through a borrowed dusty old atlas showed it to be a province in Canada and not some fancy country I had somehow missed out on. And then, before I'd even heard of some place called Toronto, I learned of, as we all did, of another T-word — Tax. Everyone seemed to know that the taxes were very high in Canada.

It's odd, isn't it, that when your heart has made its decision,

THE 'CANADA' DREAM

nothing else matters? Canada was my dream and that's where I was going. Nothing could change that.

However, my first attempt at immigration ended even before I'd picked up a pen to fill in a form. An immigration lawyer quoted me a fancy sum and the young me, with not much of a bank balance, locked the dream away. I don't remember that day or the conversation with the lawyer but the chilling amount that was quoted froze my dream.

I do remember being a big Bryan Adams fan then. The dreamy *Summer of 69* that I loved and blasted often on my car stereo, slowly began to fade away. On a typical summer day in Oman, when everything in that sun-baked part of the earth melts, the Bryan Adams cassette, forgotten in the car, turned to a semi-circular molten mess. Most unceremoniously, I dumped it out. The dream would remain a dream, unless I won the odd jackpot in the weekend lotto played at the hotels.

It was at this time, my single life bloomed. In the desert, where life was full of show and no substance, I met, fell in love, and married Lynn. This turn of events changed a lot of things in my life. The savings began, Lynn's bigger bank balance stabilized things and, of course, her dream of immigrating to New Zealand became my stepping-stone to Canada.

The New Zealand dream I whitewashed pretty easily with the lure of Canada, of the West and the US right next door. I was a *techie*, of course, and "a Canadian citizenship and the US jobs and dollars right there" was the argument that finally won her over. I'm sure I hinted at the quiet New Zealand life, the lonely farms and the sheep. Even if it was a fleeting rumor, I made sure I gave it enough legs to seal my Canadian dream.

Coming to Canada 33

Coming to Canada

Here's a thought for the millions who

are born here, grow up here, and for whom citizenship and the privilege to live in this country has come naturally. Count it as a lotto 649 that you won at birth. For the hundreds and thousands who come through a long, hard immigration process, it is a lifetime of work, forms, documents, long wait times, struggle, money, bank accounts, savings and, ultimately, success. Our first visit to an immigration lawyer, recommended by a friend, felt like a visit to the ocean's edge. We could see the endless sea ahead and hear about the pot of gold on the other side. We were just starting the swim across. There was nothing tangible to hold on to, just a chat and then back to regular routines. There were no promises made, a ton of forms to fill, a warning of an evaluation, a likely interview, a waiting period and, of course, in dollar terms, a few thousands. If you were a depressed person looking for an easy fix, this was not the lift you were looking for — an instant ticket to Canada or away from the Middle East. It would be a long and testing journey and not until the very end would we have sight of the *Promised Land*.

By this time, I was eagerly reading and soaking up every little detail about the country that was to be our new homeland. I found it fascinating — from Brian Mulroney and Pierre Trudeau to 110 volts, not 230. Taxes and provinces, the great lakes from the geography books were suddenly coming alive. The Niagara Falls would soon be more than a picture postcard. The thought of living in one of the richest and freest countries in the world was a thrill beyond all measure.

What would it be like? Dollars from anything you touched, and fancy living? Those were beautiful dreams and as months went by the land on the other side of the ocean slowly took shape. The rigid evaluation process, the ultra strict medical tests and the requirement of a healthy bank balance, all made it seem worth our while. It gave us the assurance of something really good on the other side, that we were paying our fair due to live in one of the best countries in the world.

Toronto, at that time, had been voted one of the best cities in the world to live and work in, sadly always way lower in the ranks than Vancouver. When my wife Lynn mentioned a cousin who lived in Toronto, Canada's economic engine, or better still the Bombay of Canada, we'd found a new city to call home, though with a very funny name, Toronto.

The internet, especially in the Middle East was still in its infancy in the late 90s. *Google* did not exist and our first search on *Yahoo* revealed a picture of the CN tower. Our later searches were more on *Monster.com* and *Jobshark.com* and gradually the thought of the big gulf we had to cross began to become a reality.

We weren't disheartened. On the rare days when it rained, and the cool dark clouds covered the Sun's hot unending blaze, Lynn and I would snuggle up and dream of beautiful Canada, and the good life ahead. For us, it was an experience straight out of an *X-Files* set and our *Summer of 69* would be a glorious one.

I say it again: an immigrant's journey to Canada is long and hard. It calls for a total life change, a long bureaucratic application process that ends up involving everything. It means uprooting yourself completely from where you are to move a new land where you own nothing, have nothing, and start at the very bottom. If, like us, you are lucky to have relatives in Canada, you have a familiar smiling face helping you get a bit of a foothold before you jump headlong into Canadian life. I've heard of some brave souls who land here knowing no one and ready to start a new life with just the name of some cheap hotel that a taxi driver has recommended.

Yet how many remember that moment when that plane touched down and they took their first steps into Canada. It is probably defined more by the tension and the nervousness of what lies ahead. And in the immediate hours ahead, wondering if all the paper work was good enough, would they put you right back on the next plane, branded an illegal alien? As I stood in line to see an immigration officer, separated from the rest of the passengers by a very smiling airport agent, I took in my first sights of Canada. The immigration offices, then, were right next to the customs office, next to the red channel, the place where your suitcases are opened and white-gloved customs officers dig through your baggage. Thankfully, the suitcases were not mine. But the sight was enough to have me nervously checking my right of landing form, passport, cards, and all other documents all over again.

As I sat the immigration officer probably sensed my nervousness and gave me a big smile. "Welcome to Canada", he said, genuinely. "Thank you", I replied, thinking I would feel even better if he did what he had to do and said, "Ok, you're through. It was over soon enough and, with the biggest smile, I said thank you and marched into a beautiful summer evening in the land that was to be my new home.

It felt good as Gavin, Lynn's cousin, drove me to his home. I sat back in his car and relaxed, feeling really good. The long immigration process was finally coming to an end. Somewhere along the way we saw some fireworks and the festive nature of that evening felt like a big welcome to my new home.

It did not take me long to discover that Canadians are good people. So says the world, and indeed we are. I got confirmation of that pretty soon. A few days after I'd landed Lynn was to follow with our year-old son, Nathan. Gavin was to pick us up at the airport. Having left him a rushed message on his phone about a timing mix up, I called right back apologizing for the rushed message. "You were born to be a Canadian", Gavin told me. How nice, I thought, I guess I belong here.

So, finally, the Promised Land! Every immigrant, who has made the conscious choice, feels the thrill as each new day one moves a step closer to settling in.

Like most Canadians, I instantly fell in love with the summer, even though I had just come from a place where summer was the equivalent of our winter! There was so much happening, road shows, street festivals, fairs, amusement parks, camps and cottages. The beautiful and quiet treelined streets, big houses, cars stopping to let you pass, unimaginable back home in India, smiling people and, of course, hot dogs at my first Blue Jays game. It felt like a city in celebration. Simple little sights and actions became ingrained into a beautiful feeling stored in my memory forever — riding the TTC, learning the dos and don'ts of transfers, walking the Skywalk to the Convention Centre, the sight of beautiful lake Ontario, a GO train rolling out of Union Station, and the majestic CN tower. Coming to Canada felt good even though the anxieties of starting a new life slowly began to make their presence felt.

A Canadian Conscience 39

A Canadian Conscience

O Canada, the national anthem we sing so often always with a tinge of emotion in our hearts, always inspires. And Canada, our beloved country, rarely disappoints. However, for those whose dreams fail to realize to full measure, it's a struggle. Many Canadian-born citizens, too, do not enjoy the benefits our rich nation can give. For them, too, it is sometimes a long struggle. And, those who miss out on the benefits of prosperity have to choose between heating, shelter or food, — the basics of life that are taken for granted by most Canadians.

In an age dominated by audio-visual media, a Habitat for Humanity advertisement titled *Food or Shelter* conveys this better than a million words. The simple commercial shows the roof getting ripped off as the lady in that kitchen opens a can of soup. And then the roof falls back on as she closes back the lid of that untouched can of soup. At first it may fool you into thinking it a super dramatic ad for the power contained in the can of soup that is being opened. Super-Soup? Power-of-veggies? Fat-free-pasta… Your mind keeps guessing. Before you irritatedly ask, "Ok, so what's it about?" you notice the woman's melancholic expression and a simple caption that says, 'Food or shelter'? That's when you realize, that she has a choice between food and shelter. Have your home or have a meal; pay the bills or feed the kids; real decisions that need to be made. Yes, for many in our country, the choice is not between soup and pasta, but rather between soup and shelter?

Many of us embrace the goodness we find in Canada, love it, cherish it, and then forget about it, taking it for granted as so much a part of life in Canada. Those who enjoy the prosperity the most, whether by hard work or inheritance, have a responsibility to ensure that the ones left behind also share in these riches.

Canada, the good nation, always loved, never hated, envied, not despised, gives us an identity of being known as good people. In any walk of life there's always a challenge to make the good even better, and the better the best. This is the challenge before Canadians.

Good health may have the little niggles. Along with the best come the little faults. With freedom of spirit comes the risk of bondage. Canadians, too, face the risk of that little niggle, fault, and bondage turning into deeper issues of concern. It's an invitation as in any walk of life to hop off our laurels and confront our failures. For some this may be just a thought or a concern. For others it could become a passion, an agenda, an ideal, or even a rage or a cause for revolution.

I remember an old sermon about someone complaining about a torn shoe until he saw a person who had lost a foot. Freedom is precious to someone who has lived in actual bondage. Riches and wealth mean that much more to someone who has lived in poverty. Freedom of speech and action means a lot more to one who has faced actual persecution and censorship.

We read about it, in the history books, in the news and, if we are lucky, from someone who has actually faced it.

We have learned about Nelson Mandela and Mahatma Gandhi, but the experience of talking to even one person who may have been tortured and beaten for a religious or political belief brings the truth home even more.

Poverty is not a just stark reality but a way of life for anyone who has lived in a country like India. On our first vacation from Canada back to my home in India, I remember taking my son to a lunch, sponsored by my parents, at one of Mother Teresa's ashrams. It was a home where the Sisters cared for the most destitute and abandoned. They had infants a few weeks' old, as well as very elderly residents; patients with Aids, the mentally challenged and many others who had been abandoned by society.

My son, just 6 years old, had grown up in Canada. He had no idea what lay ahead. In typical Indian fashion, the residents sat on the floor, on stone benches or any little place that the tree-shaded courtyard offered. I watched the utter silence and shock on my son's face as we started serving the meals. Gently, my Dad explained to my son what was happening and told him little stories about each of the residents there. I thanked God for that experience for I knew surely that that day my son had learned a lesson about life that no number of images or lectures could teach.

I love the TV programs that charity organizations air asking for sponsorship for kids in poor nations in Africa, Asia and elsewhere. I love them because they give me opportunities to show my kids what they have and what so many others don't. I remember an incident when my son, at the age of 8, kept asking for an extra controller for his *XBox 360*. As good as any lawyer, his persistent questions and reasons seemed to fly at will. His arguments reached a peak when, realizing that he was not getting through to me, he said, "What's another $60 dollars?" I knew then, at that moment, that the lesson of the ashram had been lost amidst the riches and comforts of life here.

If we peek into our refrigerators, and then think of the many who are less fortunate than us, we'll find the contrast stark. We don't just have a lot of food. We have varieties of it, whether it is bread or ice cream. We have brown, rye, seven grain, twelve grain, white with whole grain, and a host of different kinds of bread. If you were to try and count the varieties of bagels and waffles, you would lose count.

The comparison here is not with those poor kids in Africa, whose single-room mud houses alone would be the size of four to five of our giant refrigerators put together. Rather, right here, in this land of *milk and honey* as I like to call it, there are kids that actually go hungry.

I remember the years before the 2008-2009 recession —and they came around often enough — when the government declared a surplus of a few billions. Think about it for a moment. Doesn't it make you feel rich? *Our* Government, *our* money and *our* country, after all. Maybe the connection between those billions and a few dollars worth of cereal in some poor kids' bowls may seem farfetched. But is it so difficult to use just a tiny bit of these billions to totally lift the poor children of this country out of poverty? Or, to make sure that all our kids are guaranteed their meals, daily? Is it too farfetched to think of getting every homeless person off the street? To get health care for every kind of ailment that afflicts our nation? Somewhere along the line we have settled into a comfort zone, happily content that all is well. The bad? Well, it will get fixed in time. And, somebody else will fix it.

Remember the typical fight we've all had at one stage or another, as kids, when someone stole our candy. One of the favorite words at the end of a fight was *conscience*. I guess we'd learned about *guilty consciences* rather too well in our catechism classes and adapted it rather well too. '"Guilty conscience pricks the mind"', we'd say to the kid who stole our candy. Did it really? It probably just gave him a taste to come back for more. So, do we, each one of us, even if we have acquired our wealth through sheer hard work and struggle, do we need to start thinking about a *conscience* that feels for what is not right all around us?

What would it take to get us out of our cozy corners and take a good look at the bad and the ugly? What would it take to get us to take a look at all that does not work? Maybe what we need is a revolution. Though talk of revolution may sound strange to Canadians, is it possible? Will anyone dare talk about it? We read about it in history books, perhaps as a novelty found in South America, Africa, or even Asia. As Canadians, we love to show solidarity and offer support for any cause that identifies with liberty and human rights, but we never ever dare to dream it for ourselves.

Here's a thought. As the price of oil shot through the roof in 2007-2008, everyone got hurt by it, and every single one of us felt the pinch. In less than two years, oil went from thirty six dollars a barrel to sixty five dollars a barrel and then through 100 and almost to 150! It hurt airlines, transport, the auto Industry and, for most of us, our grocery bills. The oil companies raked in billions of dollars in profit. A year's profit forecasts were sometimes met in just the first quarter. It was not a secret. Everyone knew it, and the media and the markets highlighted it in great measure. Well, someone decided to do something about it and then maybe not. Someone decided that it would be novel to boycott a single oil company for a day and hurt them a bit. Would it? Emails were written, sent and got forwarded. Hundreds were reached. They read the messages and said "Nice!" Did the proposed boycott ever get anywhere or make a difference? Not likely.

What would have happened in Asia or in a country like India where a *bandh*, literally a *closure*, would have brought the nation to a standstill? We live in a free market, yet we have traded our power of thought and action for niceness and the comfort that we would somehow find the extra dollar somewhere or simply cut back and wait it out. Did we Canadians ever dare to take on *Big Oil*? Did those big oil companies, good as they are, generators of wealth for the nation, share a generous part of a billion with any needy cause and wipe out that malaise from existence?

That's a challenge and invitation that I'd like to pose through these coming chapters. Hang on. Stay with me and let's think out a new Canadian conscience. One that enjoys the goodness, yet never loses sight of the not so good. One that is rich, yet never forgets about the many pockets of poverty that still exist.

Every nation has its rich and poor. Are the rich are bad? NO. They've probably earned and deserved every dollar in their pocket thanks to their hard work and enterprise. Yet, I'm not advocating the Robin Hood approach of robbing the rich and giving to the poor. Rather, what we need is the *equality for all* approach so well embodied in our health care system. We need a conscience that is not the prerogative or birthright of what we call the left, or the Reds, or the revolutionaries, or people in another land. It is rather a duty entrusted to everyone who has.

Check out the Habitat for Humanity ad at this address:

http://habitat.ca/foodorshelterp1105.php

Some Ugly Canadian Issues

The Shameful Reality: Poverty   49

The Shameful Reality: Poverty

What is a *malaise?* *Wikipedia* defines it as a feeling of general discomfort or uneasiness, an "out of sorts" feeling, often the first indication of an infection or other disease. *Malaise* is often defined in medicinal research as a "general feeling of being unwell". This usage may have originated in folk medicine, but it is adopted from the French word meaning "discomfort," "feeling faint," "feeling sick." So is the very existence of poverty in a rich country like ours a *malaise?* Does Canadian society as it exists today feel any sense of discomfort, of unease, or even a sense of incompleteness?

For an answer to that question, look at any current headlines in a newspaper, or the *Globe and Mail* online, *CP24,* or even *Google News Canada*. How many times do you read the word *poverty?* Do you see headlines such as "39 per cent believe they're pay cheques from poverty", "Majority want leadership on poverty", or "Rich Canadians getting richer, poor making less" or "Canada's poverty and inequality rates now higher than in most developed countries" or "Income gap widens between Canada's rich and poor" or "Poverty inequality rates jump in Canada" or "A measure of poverty", and so on?

Change the focus to health care and, alongside general health issues, do you see news items such as "Report finds poor more likely to be hospitalized", "Poor Canadians more prone to physical, mental ailments", or simply "Poor more likely to end up in hospital?" So where did the word poverty spring from when talking about health care? Are we not the envy of our rich neighbours down south who when asked for one reason they'd want to live in Canada answer, "Health Care"? We could pick a ton of issues from these sentences that make us feel ashamed. Why even go to the end of the sentence that says "Poor Canadians more prone to physical and mental ailments"? Simply look at the first two words, *Poor Canadians*. Does that feel right?

Let's shift the focus to the most vulnerable of our society, our young children. We have all watched over our little children after tucking them into bed. We watch them fall off to sleep in a minute at the end of a regular busy school day. It gives us a sense of peace. It gives us a sense of pride. It gives us a sense of feeling successful simply because we can provide for them, abundantly, day after day. It creates in us a sense of uneasiness thinking of the dangers that lurk out there. It makes us feel like a superman ready to defend our little ones. As we recall a few last words before those eyelids finally fell shut and the little chatter-mouths finally took a break for the day just ended, we find ourselves saying a million yeses. Yes to the juicy double burger, yes to that extra toy, and yes to that extra toonie for a bag of chips from school the next day.

Then picture a cold bedroom where a child has fallen asleep on a half-empty stomach. Picture a parent having to rush a child to sleep simply because there isn't enough to eat, or a parent that dreads the morning to come because the kids may have to go to school without a bite. Stop for a minute and imagine the state of mind of a parent in a grocery checkout line who has to debate between milk and bread or between cookies or potatoes. Imagine the plight of a parent who traverses those aisles of food hoping to pick up as much as possible with a few measly dollars, wondering whether they have enough to buy everything for the week or make do with whatever they can squeeze in. Imagine the plight of a parent whose weekly trip for groceries means a trip to the *Food Bank*.

Words can be so deceptive and easily read and passed over. So, to the billionaire, millionaire, and to the regular middle class parent, the reality still stands, "Picture your child without a toast, a waffle, or a bowl of cereal, or just a plain old cup of milk to start the day, simply because it is not possible".

Is this then a matter of shame or is it a tragedy? Maybe *malaise* is a really apt word as it denotes a feeling of being unwell, but liveable — the scratchy throat that tells you that, despite the vaccine, sanitizers, hand washing, and however much you tried to prevent it, the virus has finally got you. You know it will knock you down for a while and then go away.

So, have we got knocked down for the past 15 or 20 years and then decided we can limp along? Don't we realize that a limp hurts? That, in time, a limp gets painful, causes your knee to get damaged, maybe then requiring a costly orthotic, or a visit to a specialist? Are we really hurting enough to slow down and tell ourselves that instead of gingerly marching along with life we now need to take a pit stop, make doctors' appointments, or take emergency measures as soon as we can?

Allow me to introduce you to one set of statistics and a report. In November 2008, an *Ontario Association of Food Banks* report said that failure to address the root causes of poverty was costing Ontario $13 billion a year[i]. A great professor once advised me to first check to find out who sponsored a study, before I relied on it. Well, for the sceptics, even if the Association of Food Banks sponsored the study, would it make more sense if another official government report told you that poverty was costing you directly as much as $2,895 a year? The total cost of poverty for Ontario, the province with the largest population, is equal to 5.5% to 6.6% of

Ontario's GDP. And the federal and provincial governments lose between $10.4 to $ 13.1 billion dollars each year because of poverty.

Make Poverty History. These are fascinating words, amazingly put together. Whoever came up with that little catch phrase deserves a prize. Well, it represents a stellar organization, as well. In December 2008, their website proudly hosted a page that said, "Such a bold step deserves a thank you; send a message to the Government of Ontario now". So, why did Dalton McGuinty and his liberals deserve such thanks from an organization that would normally have been criticising them? *Breaking the Cycle: Ontario's poverty reduction strategy* is a 45-page government document that lists out, in detail, concrete plans to reduce poverty[ii]. Interestingly, it carries the word *conviction*, a government's conviction that it can break the cycle of poverty. This plan, the first of its kind, appropriately applauded, spoke of *reducing* poverty. How about eliminate, abolish, or destroy? Pretty strong words.

Go a step further. Here's a quote from the document:

> *Targets and Measures*
>
> *The strategy sets a target of reducing the number of children living in poverty by 25 per cent over the next 5 years. That means that while all low-income families will see the benefits of this strategy, our target will be to move 90,000 kids out of poverty*[iii].

So, what happens to the remaining 75% over the next five years? Do the words "move 90,000 kids out of poverty" stump you for a while? If not, then think of the remaining 270,000 kids still waiting. Is it ok for these 270,000 to grow up in poverty? Is it okay to tell the next generation that they may be the next 90,000 to be lifted out of poverty?

While we may want to thank the government for such a huge

THE SHAMEFUL REALITY: POVERTY

favour to our poor kids, it is not enough? Governments like to boast using terms such as *doubling the fund, tripling the grant*, etc. So, why not boast about wanting to totally eliminate child poverty? What would happen?

The answer to our question lies in the same document:

> *If child poverty were eliminated in Ontario, the additional income tax revenue for Ontario would be between $1.3 billion and $1.6 billion annually*[iv].

So says page 8 of the document called *Breaking the Cycle: Ontario's poverty reduction strategy*.

Do you think it's an unhappy omen when a child goes to school hungry? It is because that child then grows up disadvantaged in mind and body. That child then thinks of food to satisfy a hungry stomach rather than pay attention to the lesson being taught. That child's brain then does not function well enough to grasp that lesson. In time, then, that child has an IEP, and an IPRC, or many similar tools we have developed. In time, a Vice Principal then dedicates all his or her working hours towards the suspension and expulsion of that child, instead of educating that child.

Subsequently, when we have exhausted the set of steps defined in our failure manual, what happens to that child – after the suspension and expulsion, so well defined and articulated in our education act? It then makes sense that report after report suggests that the government has to invest heavily in areas such as childhood development, programs to improve school performance, higher education for at-risk youth, and in language training and workforce integration for new immigrants. Research also shows that failing students perform badly because they don't get the best of educators, the best being given to the best. Research also shows that these educational institutions cost more than institutions for regular students. And research also shows that the funds directed to the really needy are barely more than those given to regular students. I once knew a school principal who described his shock one day as he picked up his morning coffee at the local Tim Horton's drive-through on his way to school. Imagine his shock when he realized that the teen selling that coffee was the kid he had expelled the previous week. So, who should have been on their way to school that morning, the principal or the teen?

As a rich and educated society, we have invested not just in our education but also in the research surrounding it. As a learned society, we have done our homework, seen that research, and added more classrooms to our universities, for more research. We have passed on that knowledge to those that manage our government, our society, and our schools and universities.

One of the most beautiful aspects of migrating to a country you choose to go to is that it becomes your dream country, no matter what the reality. When it is a rich country, a developed nation, a technically and an industrially advanced nation, the dream becomes an awesome one. Your mind develops a picture of a perfect nation. In keeping with human nature, one totally blanks out the not so good. It's the old adage that *love is blind.* Well, stretch it a lot more to other pursuits and you'll see the picture.

And so, the Canada I dreamed about, the Canada I saw in those beautiful picture postcards, the Canada of beautiful countryside's, magnificent cities of concrete surrounded by greenery and, of course, not to forget the Canada of my *X-files.* This was the Canada I dreamed of and worked to come to. It was after all one of the richest countries in the world, a country I had worked hard to qualify for, to come and live in. The immigration dream always harboured the fear

THE SHAMEFUL REALITY: POVERTY

that this was a big life test and that any day a call from the immigration agent would say we had been rejected.

Yes, we passed the test, came to Canada, beautiful as ever, rich as ever, loving, kind and generous as ever. A Canada so good that I don't remember when I started discovering the not so good. Sure, it didn't take me long to discover that crime and shootings were a part of life. That was easy, visible everywhere. Prejudice, bias, discrimination, and some other more personal discoveries were different.

I recall, within a few months, challenging other immigrants who spoke of racial prejudice and of many other forms of discrimination that they faced. In reality and from my real experience, nowhere had I been accepted and treated better than in this country. Early on, walking on College Street in Toronto with my first colleagues and seeing the poor, the drug addicts by the roadside, and the poor soliciting outside subway stations, I learned about people living on welfare. That came with a lot of bias. "That's a choice", I heard someone say. That, and the fact that in a few weeks I was succeeding so well in a technologically and industrially advanced country, led me to believe that no way could anybody be living on the fringes of society. "If they want, they can make it too", so many friends and colleagues told me.

One of my most vivid memories that go with it is of one of my earliest colleagues Jay. Jay, Debbie, a bunch of others, and I, were then working as consultants for the Toronto District School Board. We were all self-employed IT consultants who were masters of our trades. It was a tech savvy bunch with expertise of various kinds thrown in. Jay was one of the most brilliant of the bunch with his skills in *UNIX*, *Perl*, and various other tough scripting skills. "Watch as my hands never leave my fingers", he would say, as people would stare in awe how his one line *UNIX* commands would work magic.

I guessed then that all that talent and intelligence really paid well too. Well, on our daily trips for smokes and, of course, to *Starbucks* or *Second Cup*, Jay would have a hand full of toonies ready. He always had a toonie for any man, woman or kid that came with their little coffee cups. "Bums", he would lovingly call them and drop in his toonie. He also always explained, "That's to make sure that if I am in that state one day, people will do the same for me". It convinced me even more that in this country there was no substitute for hard work and that you always made it, to one side or another.

Well, I did discover poverty in some pretty brutal ways. I don't remember the when, but the faces of the people that stood in line on bitter cold days outside the synagogue near my home, just to get a bit of food, was not a pleasant sight. Aptly or ironically, it was called the *Out of the Cold* program. Later, as I took up a course and started classes downtown in the not so busy hours, I discovered so much more. On cold days with minus 20 degrees temperatures, discovering bundles that were supposedly human on the grills that spewed out hot air, exhausts from those money generating downtown offices, was a sad experience.

I remember being transfixed by one particular old man as I huddled and walked past, trying to look not too obvious with my stares. He knew it and looked in my direction, as well, I guess hoping for a loonie or something. "Sir, can you spare me something," he asked, almost cynically. If you are new to an English-speaking country that word sir will shock you. If you are a new immigrant still looking for a foothold then it will shock you even more if it comes from a poor person huddled up on a frozen street of a rich country. More likely, it will depress you.

I don't remember what I found in my pocket that day to give him, but it was depressing and I began to discover a

THE SHAMEFUL REALITY: POVERTY

very different face of Canada. It was the dotcom era and millionaires were popping up by the dozens. I had a dream, too, never about the millions but about my trade and how good it felt. When the dotcom bubble burst in 2001, I remembered Jay's words and hoped there would not be too many more that would have fallen off to depend on the toonies.

So, who are the poor in Canada? They are defined in various ways, technically, by their income or the lack of it; by *Revenue Canada* figures in a different way; by the media in many ways, depending on whether they need a good story or to showcase famous personalities that take up these causes in various ways. Even the actual definition of who is poor is debated.

Poverty can be restrictive or inclusive, absolute or relative. There are other poverty-related terminologies that include terms like *consumption basket*, *equity-based*, and *mixed consumption* and *equity-based measures*. A simple *Google* search on poverty in Canada will list scores of articles, each with real solutions, and lots of real people examples. Yet, it is a simple fact that line-ups at Canadian food banks and emergency shelters have grown since the 90s. From 1989 to 2000, usage of food banks grew by over 96%, as reported by *Hunger Count 2000*.

The poor, so visible in our thoughts, writings, and conscience! So, is there something being done about it? Yes. Is it enough? No. So, what do we need? How can the efforts of so many organizations and individuals not yield the results that we seek? They sure do. But then they are the stories of fish given to the hungry, much needed, but what happens in the long run?

It's amazing how Canadians give so much, and in plenty, to causes for the poor. The *Toy Mountain* for poor kids at Christmas, the *give-a-kid-a-coat* campaign, the extra toonie you paid after checking out your groceries, and the frantic campaigns when the food banks run low, are great efforts that keep the warmth and effort alive. Most of all, they keep the keep issue alive year after year. They keep those hungry people alive and they keep alive the thought that a lot of help is needed.

Is government the answer? Here is a simple thought. As I believe and hold in my heart, big revolutions, real solutions, begin from the simple answers to problems. During the economic downturn of 2008-2009, not just the US, the entire world slipped into recession and financial turmoil, governments rushed in with billions of dollars to keep their economies alive and to keep the big banks and businesses from falling into bankruptcy. There was real concerted action in real time with meetings between the G20 leaders, meetings between their finance ministers.

However, the most visible force was the resolve, implicit and explicit, of governments to keep the world from falling into recession. While the US had their giant 700 billion-dollar package and others that followed, our safer economy needed smaller boosts, 25 billion and then 50 billion and then something for the auto industry, and so on. The Government even promised to back the warranties of new cars, if *GM* and *Chrysler* went bankrupt, and ultimately ended buying an actual stake in *Chrysler* as part of the bailout. The cost to the taxpayers — a few billions!

Herein lies the answer. Why cannot a government run for four years with a simple agenda such as *Humanity in Canada*? Sure, that would be a vague definition and there would be other pressing needs, but if a government ran for four years with a focus on Canadians, what would happen? We would see miracles in real life. A government that swore to eradicate poverty and child hunger, and worked dedicatedly towards

THE SHAMEFUL REALITY: POVERTY

it, would for sure write its name in history, and a country so uplifted by this one critical issue would solve not just this one issue but numerous ones. A country energized by its people would be a country on the move. How many billions would it cost? As for any solution, what would we need? We would need an immediate solution, *First Aid* for the debilitated (vulnerable, weakened) part of the Canadian body, and a long-term solution, the long-term care that would provide the poor with education, jobs, and a resolve to keep rising. Does a government have this solution or does any particular political party have it?

It's in the hands, in the conscience, of the people of Canada. It's in a collective will that would say, let's deal with it and let's deal with it now! It needs just one government to focus its energy on this issue, provide the means, bring the experts and the front line workers all to the table, and there will be a way. The hands on the ground, the social workers that work with the poor, and the financial and policy experts to create the long term solutions, businessmen and industrialists who would create the jobs, academics and scholars who would create the learning paths and the training and, above all, just one government with a will.

Can we do it? Yes! Is it possible? Yes! Do we have the means to do it? Yes! Do we have the wealth to do it? Yes! Do we have the resources to do it? Yes! Do we have the knowledge to do it? Yes! Do we have the people to do it? Yes! BUT, do we have the resolve to do it, now? NO! AND, do we have the leadership to do it? NO!

The Unending Tragedy: Child Poverty   63

The Unending Tragedy: Child Poverty

Death, disease, sickness, violence,

crime and war, all sicken us. The images, so vividly captured by modern technology, flash before us everywhere, on the internet, in magazines and newspapers, and in the variety of media available to us today. We now even watch wars live, beamed into our living rooms, as they happen. In all this, nothing hits home harder than the image of a suffering child. All of us have seen such images, from the simple ones to the very graphic. Some of them we simply flip over and erase from our memory faster than the turning of a page; some we share with others, distribute, and make sure we pass them on as we see fit. However, some images remain etched, not only in our memory, but also in our consciousness, forever.

One of the most stunning images etched permanently in my mind shocked me when I saw it for the first time. It's the image of Phan Thị Kim Phúc, the little Vietnamese girl immortalized in Nick Ut's Pulitzer Prize winning picture of war. In 1972, during the Vietnam War, her village had been occupied by the North Vietnamese and, consequently, was attacked by American and South Vietnamese forces. The picture reveals a terrified, screaming, pain-stricken, naked teen running — a vivid backdrop of war behind her and her back seemingly on fire from the searing heat of a Napalm bomb. (To those who have seen that image, no amount of memory lapse will erase that from the grey cells that store that image.)

TV channels flood us with images from Africa, Asia, and South America, asking for sponsorships and donations. Images of poor African children in bare, dusty spaces outside the little huts they call home, flies on their faces and a small, seemingly empty bowl with no food in it. The predominant theme that hits us is poverty — and deprived children that the world has forgotten.

We have probably gotten so used to them that we don't even give them a second thought, hopefully because we have seen them over and over again. However, it would be such a crime if we fail to pay attention to their plight just because they live in a land, a continent, or a world far, faraway, too far to threaten our senses or our conscience.

I love the ad by *The Grocery Foundation*, an organization that brings food to hungry kids, right here in Canada. The ad is stunning not by what it says in the actual sound track that goes with it. Rather, it symbolically portrays a disgustingly true reality of situations here at home. The ad is vibrantly meaningful because it challenges us to read, pay attention to, remember, and then do something about it.

If you have a toddler, teen, or just about any school going kid, and have been through the experience of class photos, it makes it so much more real. The ad portrays a class photo being taken and the photographer addresses three different students as he gets the group shot ready. Three students that are hiding or seemingly not ready for the picture. As each one of these three kids emerges, their stark white T-shirts bear a message so unreal that it makes you feel gross for having stuffed that extra dessert after another of those full meals. Here's a transcript of that ad:

> Photographer: "Ok everybody, you in the back, come forward please".
> The boy comes forward from that hidden position with

a T-Shirt that says, 'I'm hungry'.
The Camera then moves to a little seated girl thoughtfully bent forward chin resting in her hands.

Photographer: "Sweetie, sit up please".
As the girl sits up, that now visible T-Shirt says, 'I haven't eaten all day'.
And then the camera pans over all the way to the other end of the group to another little seated girl.

Photographer: "And you on the end, could you please stand up". The girl stands up revealing a T-Shirt that says, 'I hope there's enough dinner tonight'.

I remember watching that ad on TV one night, first simply trying to recall those messages as the ad came and went. I waited for it to come again as the memory of that ad slowly sank in. I missed it a few more times as I got to bed guilty for having forgotten to look for it, too caught up with the jokes from *Leno* and *Letterman* among those late night talk shows. A reminder on the *Blackberry* helped me catch it once more, this time leaving me numb from the sad and downcast faces of those kids. I did note the time it aired and finally got it recorded.

I could have been a little wiser and simply gone to *YouTube*. It had been there all the time. And then I watched it a million times, over and over again, not knowing whether to look at the faces or the messages. It sickened me, and pained me, and then left me feeling even guiltier, just plain guilty about myself. I didn't know why. Was I supposed to feed all the hungry children of Canada, or was I responsible for them? Was it my responsibility to provide for those kids, or was it my responsibility to do something about the situation?

You can watch that ad over and over and yet not do a thing about it. If you have seen that ad or if you journeyed with me through those lines, you would realize and think that while we may talk about and discuss the pain that that ad leaves, it represents real pain in real little children that are hungry. For every night that I forgot to find that ad after seeing it once, a few thousand kids went to sleep that night, hungry. And, for every time that I saw and reflected on that ad, a little tummy growled in pain, somewhere, not in anticipation of a meal but in the realization that the hunger was real and there was no meal coming.

Yet, we live in a land where food is in abundance. We live in a land of plenty or, as I like to say, a land of billions, real billions of dollars. During the 2009 G20 summit, leaders of some of the world's richest countries gathered in London, England, to create a plan to fight the recession. Jamie Oliver, the young famous British chef who prepared some exotic meals for those Presidents and Prime Ministers at the summit, was caught in the limelight. As they interviewed him at his work, Jamie said he had once met Tony Blair the then Prime Minister of England and had complained about the quality of food in schools. Tony Blair gave him 280 million pounds to change what he saw wrong. The message? A simple one. There is money and there is a need. But do we need celebrities, each time, to highlight these issues?

I have never felt more justified and right about my move to Canada as when I have guests visiting me from overseas. Food is the centre of a party and as we get through course after course the talk invariably veers to food. I have heard comments about food being so plentiful, economical, and tasty in Canada. I have heard praises about something as simple as a loaf of bread to exotic dishes, some straight out of the microwave, entrees and varieties of desserts so easily served, consumed, relished, discussed and taken for granted. We don't just have starters for dinners, we have courses of starters, we don't just have one dish, we have varieties of them.

And desserts? We love our sweets, our chocolates, our ice creams, and our variety of desserts. We truly indulge in them.

And so, isn't it ironic that in this very land, the land of plenty, the land of milk and honey, there are children that do not have food? Just plain and simply put: In Canada, there are children without food. Let's repeat that. There are children in poor families that are hungry; children in poor families that do not know if there will be enough to eat; and children in poor families that worry where their next meal is coming from.

When I see the suffering children of the world, especially the hungry ones, I feel a sense of despair, despair easily blamed on, "that world far away", corrupt politicians, unscrupulous businessmen, unequal distribution of resources, militias, and a host of other reasons. "It is doable", I tell myself — in time, over years, maybe a few generations even.

What do you feel when you hear about the hungry children of Canada? Are you surprised, intrigued, angry, disgusted, or apathetic even? Who do you direct your feelings towards? Maybe, you blame those lazy parents who give birth and cannot work hard to provide enough or take care of their children? How about guilt? Maybe, you feel just a little bit guilty, once you've done your good deed for the week and dropped a toonie into a bowl somewhere along the street.

As an IT professional, I get to attend a lot of seminars and meetings. Most of these seminars are free, sponsored by vendors marketing their products through these presentations. Obviously, these events are well catered for, a nice breakfast, midday snacks, juice, coffee, and perhaps a nice hot lunch, too. The most fascinating sight is the later afternoon window when cookies, cereal bars and ice creams get served, all devoured by grown ups, as if they were little children in a candy park.

Take a trip to downtown Toronto. Visit a few of the many big hotels and their conference centres, full of delegates, transacting business, exchanging ideas and knowledge, and doing all the stuff that comes so naturally to those of us living in a industrialized and modern country. You may even be lucky enough to see the odd seminar on poverty, of course, at the *Sheraton*.

And, then, there are the buffets. We all love them — buffets representing every possible type of cuisine, continental, Chinese, Indian, Mediterranean, Brazilian, and a whole lot more. I love these places and cheekily try to go there on a birthday because, of course, there's a freebie for the one born that day. At one such place, there's a sign I've seen with a telling message. It says, "Even though the food is unlimited, please do not waste".

I don't mean to criticise. Rather, I take comfort from the fact that we well and truly live in a land of plenty, that we have the means to give our families those beautiful treats and enjoy the goodness of every culture, represented so well and truly through their cuisine. I cannot but think, nevertheless, of those who, in this same land of plenty, have little or no food.

While the great majority work, earn, and bring home their daily bread, there are many who still cannot. And, consequently, many little children go hungry. Each time I think of that, I stop and wonder where, how, and why? If you have travelled to any Third World nation you may have seen — as I have in my own country, India hundreds of little hungry, dirty, ragged, poor little children begging for scraps. You see these scenes vividly and then, perhaps, accept them as part of that society.

So, where are these poor and hungry children in Canada? You will not find them on the streets, or in the parks or at subway stations with their begging bowls. The *Toronto Star* once published an article called "Down, out and hidden away in Oakville"[v]. It highlights the case of Sharon, a mother of four who moved to subsidized housing to escape an abusive spouse. Her means of survival, as well as that of her four kids: the *Food Bank*! The article amazingly highlights how a poor family can be hidden away in a rich community, unseen and unheard, barely surviving. Herein lies the irony. They are well and truly hidden from us, so well hidden that the majority of us could go through life peacefully without even having to face a single one of them. They are so well hidden that, as I dare to repeat here, we could go through government after government, question period after question period, election after election, ad after ad, year after year of surpluses, measured in the billions, and yet not notice the painful reality that — and I'd sadly like to repeat this — so many children in Canada go hungry, so many children in Canada get maybe just one meal a day, or so many children in Canada wonder if there will be any food on the table tonight, or wonder where their next meal will come from.

In 2002, Greg deGroot-Maggetti, Coordinator for *Citizens for Public Justice*, wrote a paper titled "A measure of poverty in Canada"[vi]. In the paper, he quotes the responses of children to a poignant question, "What does poverty mean?"

As we browse through those responses, each one of us will hopefully identify them with one or more of our own experiences, or with some point that really drives home the stark reality in those answers. Some we'll probably bypass and say ok, some we'll analyze as technical, standard or elementary for a child, but some will bring our world to a dead stop. Or, would they?

Here are the responses:-

Poverty Is...

Not being able to go to McDonald's
Getting a basket from the Santa Fund
Feeling ashamed when my dad can't get a job
Not buying books at the book fair
Not getting to go to birthday parties
Hearing my mom and dad fight over money
Not ever getting a pet because it costs too much
Wishing you had a nice house
Not being able to go camping
Not getting a hot dog on hot dog day
Not getting pizza on pizza day
Not being able to have your friends sleep over
Pretending that you forgot your lunch
Being afraid to tell your mom that you need gym shoes
Not having breakfast sometimes
Not being able to play hockey
Sometimes really hard because my mom gets scared and she cries
Not being able to go to Cubs or play soccer
Not being able to take swimming lessons
Not being able to afford a holiday
Not having pretty barrettes for your hair
Not having your own private backyard
Being teased for the way you are dressed
Not getting to go on school trips[7].

"Pretending that you forgot your lunch" and "not having breakfast sometimes". I read those two and then reread them and then tried to come up with one recollection of something similar in my life. Sure, I did not have breakfast many times, skipped it, because the lavish meal the previous night should have seen me through a week. It made me sick at the thought of the options a hungry child faces. Does that child sit at lunchtime and stare at the others having their lunch, feel the pit of an empty stomach and the saliva in their mouth from the lack of food?

If you dare to, try it one day as you rush to the food court with a ravishing hunger, ready to dig into that foot-long *Sub*. Don't buy it. Pretend. Just sit in that noisy food court, take in all the aromas, look at the visual beauty of the food, Chinese, Indian, Greek, or whichever fascinates you, and then feel the pain of hunger at not being able to eat. No sane Canadian who swears by everything that is Canadian, be it human rights, equality, justice, etc., can do that and feel assured that all is well.

As that child sits there, does he or she hope for someone to share or, alternatively, does that child get his or her first lesson in panhandling or begging? Does that child get his or her first thoughts of stealing or of resentment towards the injustice of it all? It is a simple thought that any Prime Minister or Premier could read about and make a priority.

From 1989 onwards, federal politicians have been pledging to eradicate child poverty by the year 2000. Yet, twenty years later, poverty still exists. Child hunger still afflicts those little stomachs. So, what's more real or painful, child soldiers in Africa, child workers in South America and Asia, or hungry children in Canada? We would probably choose the child soldier in Africa and start a movement and organization for their cause. We would then easily raise funds, probably rake in thousands of dollars, support a few villages, buy them goats, and help them with clean water, textbooks, pencils and schools. We would help rehabilitate those lost children. Even television stations would happily air special features on them. All very good and noble, but year after year we would still continue to forgive and let our political leaders survive on their failed promises to the littlest and frailest ones in our society.

Who do we blame? The government? Easy, and so true. Isn't it the responsibility of that same body that collects all those taxes and has all those surpluses, to provide for these little ones? Every government easily reels off statistics, passes bills, and points out measures and initiatives taken to tackle this problem. There's no shortage of measures taken. Indeed, the list is long. So, then, why do children in Canada still go hungry?

> Check out the Grocery foundation ad at this address:
>
> http://www.youtube.com/watch?v=arejqsw_DxQ

Canada's own Third World Nation 75

Canada's own Third World Nation

My personal journey of discovery of

the First Nations and their plight was long delayed. As a new immigrant, I had found the same biased half-truths that I had heard about the poor, the unemployed and those left behind. I had little idea who the natives were, where they were and, for that matter, what their conditions were. The only picture in my mind was the one I had seen in movies and all those cowboy comics and they were not very friendly depictions. Kevin Costner's *Dances with Wolves*, during one of its reruns on TV, came as a handy reminder of a deeper reality that existed.

There is no mandated education for landed immigrants. And the little booklet about Canada one studies for the citizenship test is a sketchy lesson on the history of this land. The rosy picture I had of the original inhabitants of this land, now living a protected life, slowly faded as news articles of neglect, poverty, and suffering came to my attention. And it left me wondering how many Canadians travel through life without so much as a thought about the real issues that afflict these people.

I must confess, however, that my deeper realization of this reality arrived when I was working on this actual chapter. As I discovered this unfortunate and forgotten Canada, I jumped passionately into doing something about it. Writing seemed such a logical expression of the frustration and anger at the unrealized potential of so much that could be made to happen for all Canadians. And so, I wrote chapter after chapter on poverty, child poverty and hunger, crime, sports, and on so many other issues. One of the first persons I discussed my book with, a very passionate Canadian, told me that no book of this kind could ever be complete without a mention of how the natives of this land have been robbed of everything they had and left at the very bottom of the ladder, poor, and deprived. "Ok, I will include a chapter on the First Nations," I remember telling him feeling pretty satisfied with myself and relishing the thought of a new chapter on something so critical. His answer was a very vehement and stern, "No! Write two chapters!"

As I researched the issue guiltily, drawing on my memory of events over my decade's stay in Canada, it struck me that I had read about it all along, and seen it on the news. Yet, in my mind, for some vague reason, the indigenous people had never been a part of the equation. I now think, am I one of a kind or did that old me represent millions of Canadians who hardly ever give it a thought? Do we live our lives off this land and never give a thought to the ones that have lived here for centuries and then lost it all to the ones that came in later?

As I set about this chapter, I was faced with the life-stopping dilemma of where to begin. Should I jump right into the inhuman conditions of these people now, or go way back in history to 1200 B.C. and begin there? Ultimately, I based my decision on a sense of optimism and started looking for the good, for the pillars of this community who have transcended their own afflictions in order to right this terrible wrong. And so, I set about looking at the First Nations through the eyes of two towering historical figures: Phil Fontaine, a native Canadian, and Archbishop Desmond Tutu, a pillar of history who lived through and saw one of the most shameful chapters of humanity, *apartheid*, rewritten.

Chief Phil Fontaine:

In A *salute to Phil Fontaine*, June 2009[viii], Andy Scott, former federal minister for Indian and Northern Affairs, called Chief Fontaine an irreplaceable leader and a formidable partner. When Phil Fontaine chose to retire in the summer of 2009, people from all walks of life, especially politicians, both current and former, and political pundits and commentators, unanimously agreed that we were a losing a champion. Fontaine served three terms as National Chief of the Assembly of First Nations. Most importantly, Fontaine's achievements as leader will be listed in Canadian history forever. His personal top three: the expression of sorrow from Pope Benedict XVI, the Government of Canada apology from Prime Minister Stephen Harper, and the Indian Residential Schools Settlement Agreement.

If you were to step outside and look objectively at the three issues, the one common theme you'd see without a moment's hesitation would be of a people wronged, a process of catch-up and a present still caught in a terrible past. I've discovered that Canadians are very scared of a very common human experience — saying *sorry*. As someone has said so well, "In Canada, we have held the word *sorry* to a ransom". Yet, here we were, a nation, a church and entire generations that owed the word "Sorry" to those that owned this land for not hundreds but thousands of years.

On June 13, we celebrate National Aboriginal Day. Aptly, the theme and purpose of the day is to reconcile and rebuild our relationship with our First Nations. So, in 2009, when we celebrated the 13th annual occurrence of this day, one would think we would have come a long way from those days of destitution, deprivation, and dependency, three terms found in the United Nations Commission on Human Rights report on Canada's First Nations. If those terms appear too academic, on the 13th celebration of this day, the real life reports used lay terms such as poverty, poor living conditions, and serious health issues.

Archbishop Desmond Tutu:

Looking at life through reports from news agencies always seems to create a disconnected and abstract picture. It's always the personal touch that attracts us. Archbishop Desmond Tutu, the well known bishop from South Africa, who gave the word evil a whole new meaning and pronunciation, knew poverty, suffering, and oppression, better than any leader of our times. Archbishop Tutu's horrified reaction to conditions that he saw when he visited the First Nations shows us the best way to describe the conditions, even today. He described the conditions as worse than those found in the townships of South Africa. For us, to put it in very real, stark terms, they were worse than conditions in a slum. This is our own little Third World; our own little museum of what abject poverty and deprivation is like. We preserve it, probably, to showcase it as a reminder of what has been.

We refer to our relationship with the First Nations as a tragic past, a past that we unabashedly use as an ongoing theme in all our references. As Andy Scott says, "Our nation is scarred with the betrayal and misguided, even malicious, public policy"[9]. We, as a nation, have totally accepted that here are a people whom we dispossessed of their lands, resources, and culture. Somehow we are still in the past. The present and tomorrow, despite our best efforts, are still at a murky stagnation point.

If you were to walk into a slum in any Third World nation you would see open drains, sewers, and shanty houses, black rivers of nauseous gases and garbage, filthy conditions and poor malnourished children with ailments of every kind. Sadly, for so many of my friends here in Canada, the realization of that reality has struck home not from all the images of these places but from a joke by Russell Peters. His joke about what happened when they opened the door of the aircraft on landing in Mumbai, would send every Canadian scampering back into the safety of that aircraft, never to venture in that direction again. It was an exaggerated reference to the stench that would wallop you in the face. The appalling conditions in the shanty towns of India and of many Third World nations seem a world away. Given a choice between Mexico and Europe, or between the Dominican Republic and Disney Land, many Canadians may never end up travelling to those lost worlds. Here's an option. Why don't we, as part of our moral national duty, travel to those forgotten First Nations reserves and see the conditions there for ourselves?

Kids with sores, bandaged hands, backed up sewers, and boiling water advisories for more than a decade, generations that have never known running water or what it is to drink water out of a tap, mould-infested houses; families of 10-15 members living in houses crumbling from every visible angle; and numerous other conditions surely difficult to believe possible in a country that is consistently voted one of the best to live on this earth. Surely an exaggeration, you might say.

We love Africa. For some reasons, that continent has a fascination for us — the wild life, the natives, the militias, or the poor. For example, take a very basic human need such as clean drinking water. A lack of clean water there gets us donating generously. It gets a whole lot of our school kids fund raising and then making that arduous trip across the ocean to dig wells and build wind-powered water pumps. It's basic technology that can get the job done.

At the other end of the scale, we even use super advanced technology to help other countries in times of natural disaster. The Canadian DART team is an outstanding example of this. In Honduras, after the 1998 earthquake, in Turkey in 1999, and in Sri Lanka during the deadly 2004 tsunami, the DART team became a lifeline to millions who faced the fury of nature. Besides logistical and critical support, the team produced over 10 million litres of water!

Can we not use this technology for our own people? Somehow, we have forgotten our own little Third World. Here, in our own backyard, a nation of people lives in inhuman conditions. In a country steeped in technology, this little yet vital need seems a mirage. A father on one of the reserves once said, "It's like raising your children in a toilet, in a community that is a cesspool".

Three Incidents:

In October 2005, Canada woke up to the horrors of a community that showed children with horrific skin diseases like scabies and impetigo. As those images of bodies covered in rashes and scars, some of which we in our comfortable and clean homes might label as gross, flashed across the country, we rediscovered the emotions called shock and anger. Did it happen overnight? Hardly so. *E Coli* contaminated water, later loaded with chlorine, was the culprit. And so, it happened that in the 21st century, in a country called Canada, we saw a phenomenon called mass evacuation. More than a thousand residents had to be evacuated to cities like Ottawa, Sudbury, Cochrane, Timmins, Peterborough and Sault Ste. Marie.

Why? To give them access to medical care and clean water. Medical care, which for most Canadians is a walk around the block; or clean water, the realization of which would be at best a lack of enough pressure in the many jets in modern day showers.

On May 7, 2009, five-year-old Tristan Mousseau died in a house fire on the Sandy Bay Ojibwe First Nation. There were 11 people in that home, including eight children. Alvin Maytwayashing, grandfather of the boy and owner of that home, said the boy may have been forgotten in the confusion as the family escaped through a window at the back of the house. His words, "He was in the bedroom, the master bedroom, on the bed. He was sleeping but they woke everybody up. I don't know how they forgot about him. I can't really say".

In February, earlier that year on the same reserve, a grief-stricken father buried his 9-year-old daughter. The house destroyed in a fire had 15 residents. Michael Dumas, the father of nine-year-old Hope Richard could not attend the wake for Tristan Mousseau; because it would have felt like living the death of his daughter all over again. Overcrowding in those community homes was blamed for both the deaths.

In June 2009, the World Health Organization (WHO) declared the H1N1 flu a pandemic. Canada then had 3047 confirmed cases, with 5 deaths. A particular trend that caught the attention of the WHO was the rapid spread of the disease in aboriginal communities. It was not limited to a single province but was widespread across native reserves. As Dr. Donald Low, head of Ontario's public laboratory system, said,

"In some of these communities, the living standards are really a perfect breeding ground for the spread of a virus like this. You have four, five, six people living in one dwelling, not having access to clean water and not being able to wash, never mind to protect others when somebody in that family comes down with the disease".

When Alvin Maytwayashing referred to the little boy being forgotten in the confusion, it wasn't a case of *home alone*. The boy was not forgotten at home while the rest of the family went on a Christmas vacation. Here was a boy forgotten in the confusion, left in a burning home, to die.

Our greatest fear, as parents, is the dread of losing one's child. After the solid brick and concrete homes in India, my greatest fear after discovering the wood structured homes in Canada was the thought of a fire. We discussed it all the time, shivered with the thought of the possibility of one, and tried to get past that to the thought of an escape plan. My biggest fear, an actual living dread that I live with, is the thought of coming home to a burning house and realize that my children are in there, with no way in and no way out and only one outcome. When I saw the father of the little nine-year-old talk of his grief, for the first time in life, I imagined the thought for real and placed my two sons in that burning home. Would you dare to try that thought or one in which you had escaped but your child had been left behind, to die?

These three incidents are highlights, symptoms of a system that has totally failed those that have lived here forever. Here are communities with brutal living conditions. For communities beset with poverty that is way higher than for non-indigenous people, isolated on reserves, with little social and economic development, the results are almost foregone conclusions. Unemployment, sometimes as high as 75%, rampant substance abuse, health and emotional disturbance, gang activity, and so many other social phenomenon that are now a regular part of life among the First Nations. If you list words such as HIV and AIDS, suicide rate, birth defects, infant mortality, and many such health related issues, you will clearly see how much higher this rate is among the First Nations.

When Phil Fontaine retired he left with many hopes but the one he singled out was the issue of First Nations' poverty. Andy Scott, in the article referred to earlier, spoke of a "conciliatory political approach" adopted by Fontaine[10]. He believed in a spirit of collaboration, despite being a survivor of the resident schools.

If Archbishop Tutu were to come back to Canada today, what change would he see in First Nations reserves? Would he see similar appalling conditions, or look at the new world of First Nations and try and remove a distorted Canadian image from his mind? Will we see a new beginning for our First Nations? As Chief Fontaine said, "If Canada was measured by the conditions of the First Nations, we'd be 63rd on the list, not 1st; a Third World nation, not a first".

When faced with such a massive systemic failure, our first reaction is to think of the many generations it will take to right a wrong such as this. Over the years, the government has spent hundreds of millions of dollars. On the one hand, the First Nations may complain of massive injustice meted out and, on the other, government may list spending worth hundreds of millions.

When the overcrowded housing issue surfaced, Vic Toews, Manitoba's senior cabinet minister in Ottawa, was quick to point out the 400 million dollars allocated in the budget for two years and the additional housing allowances given. "A drop in a bucket", was the response from Charlie Hill, an aboriginal housing advocate.

The answer lies in letting the First Nations lead. It lies in allowing them to decide the best way forward, with all governments in full support. The Kelowna Agreement, that had all thirteen governments and five national aboriginal organizations as signatories, was a huge step forward towards improving the lives of the First Nations. It came from a collaboration of all forms of government and First Nation organizations.

Chief Fontaine's biggest push in this process was to let the First Nations lead and direct. Today, those 400 million dollars could be given out directly to contractors who would promise to train and employ First Nations people only. The First Nations would lead, decide, and allocate housing. Somewhere, thinking a little outside the box would have solutions for everyone.

How does the government react to and support the First Nations, if their conditions are so deplorable? When the *E Coli* contaminated water problem first broke out, the federal government organized a massive airlift. It shipped in bottled water and announced a plan to rebuild the complete reserve. There was an additional $300 million dollars for new homes and programs for rehabilitation. Would this create a new community, bereft of all the old social issues? A community robbed of its culture could not be rehabilitated.

How we perceive reality around us, especially with regard to the other person, determines how we judge them. In modern literature, perspective is a sexier term, preached and talked about by many great speakers. I prefer the term prejudice. It has the exact amount of negativity to it.

So, how prejudiced are we towards our native brothers and sisters? We don't need research to tell us that we are very prejudiced. It's reflected all around our society and in the conditions of the First Nations. Does it influence our thoughts, judgement, and action? Does it influence our decision-making? Does it influence us enough to hold back when lives may be at stake?

When the H1N1 flu spread rapidly through our urban communities, the response was swift. Health advisories, tips, prevention measures, literature, and up to date information flowed rapidly. Prevention and care was marketed like the magic pill. A simple daily use flu item like the hand sanitizer became the self-guard option. It was everywhere, within easy reach of anyone and everyone, at schools, malls, food courts, churches, washrooms, and all public places. We had our own stashes at our desks and work surroundings. We used sanitizers and washed our hands, both in whichever order we preferred.

'The same H1N1 flu spread even more rapidly through the native communities. That's when our health officials decided that sanitizer for the natives was not a good idea. It had some alcohol content in it that could be abused. Whether that decision was based on some much stretched logic, or on some exceptions for a small minority, people acted on that prejudice and, at the height of the H1N1, shipping out of the sanitizer to First Nations was delayed. Some chiefs drove hundreds of kilometres to buy it for their communities. Someone even proposed an even more brilliant idea. Let them just wash their hands with water and soap — in homes that have never had running water in the history of their existence!

Increasingly, we need to hand back the controls to the First Nations. Here are communities, rigidly in commune with their own culture, respect for nature and tradition, and communities led by their elders. Would this be the ideal starting point? We need to let them fix their own social and community issues, and let them lead the path to a tomorrow that is rid of these issues. We need to follow closely, with advice, funds, and support, and only then will we see a new generation of First Nations that is on par with the rest of Canada.

The first immigrants to Canada came around the 16th or 17th century. The First Nations lived here thousands of years before that, from a time we refer to as B.C. Perhaps, a task as simple as listening to the wisdom and knowledge of the people who know their own habitat best would be a great start. When government built the Kashechewan reserve, it totally ignored the advice of the local elders on the choice of location. Even before the first shovel hit the ground the elders knew the plains were prone to flooding. Today, we refer to those homes as *mould-infested* ones, thanks to that same flooding. When the James Bay water treatment plant got contaminated by *E Coli*, the cause could be determined, not through some very complicated scientific analysis but through plain common sense. The culprit: the sewage from a lagoon just 150 yards upstream. But then no one listened to the locals.

In 2009, as Governor General Michaëlle Jean toured the Arctic North, she grabbed the headlines for a variety of reasons. A bite of a seal heart, straight from a hunt sent a message across the seas to Europe stronger than any politician at a table could argue. However, another message, that she actively campaigned for, hardly got a response in Ottawa; probably a deaf ear. While some even argued it was none of her business, or of the Governor General's office, she bravely pushed it. The message: build a university in the Arctic North.

From the history of such a plan in countries like the US, Finland, Norway and Sweden, we knew it was possible. She knew it was possible. What could be greater than a university for the natives, embedded in their own culture and surroundings? A university, a single campus, or one with many satellite campuses under one umbrella, that first brought to life the very lifestyle and culture of the First Nations and then mixed it with math, sciences, engineering and medicine. This could be a university that could cater to hundreds of native youth and then invite all Canadians to join, as well. For a people, more than any race existing on this earth today, totally in communion with nature, love and respect for nature would outshine many universities simply dedicated to imparting education in buildings of brick and stone.

Phil Fontaine's achievements represent a phase of recognition and reconciliation. His work and the many issues he fought for, in a spirit of cooperation, friendship, and understanding, represent a dream for tomorrow and the way to go about it. To the ones that actually live on the reserves, the ones that face the poverty, unemployment, cramped living conditions, and a depressing tomorrow, anger and frustration is a very real sentiment. True reconciliation for these people thus will take place when real change comes to their basic standard of living. In a rich country, when basic needs such as shelter, drinking water, and work, become available to these sons and daughters of the land, that's when true reconciliation between the Canada of the cities and towns and the Canada of the reserves will take place.

A University Education for All? 91

A University Education for All?

On April 29, 2009, Louise Brown,

an education reporter, published an article entitled "Cash payments encourage college students to stay the course"[xi]. As always, nothing can be more true and enlightening as a few actual numbers. So, it would not surprise one to know that, as part of the study the article referred to, a sum of $750 dollars per term in cash reduced the school dropout rate by 35%. At risk students who were given tutoring, mentoring, and the added cash incentive, were less likely to drop out.

Naturally enough, the reactions to this kind of a study costing a "few" six million dollars or a "staggering" six million dollars, whatever your perspective, were equally opposite. There were those that threatened to quit the province and the country. For someone who must have worked hard, paid for his or her graduation, probably through hard earned dollars, precious savings, and incurred debt as well, this would be a very logical and reasonable response. There were other reactions that asked, "Why were such programs so short lived?" True enough, this was a low-income single parent and the extra cash helped pay for the student's meals — physical survival really.

A week before that report, I had completed a course in *Educational Finance and Economics* at OISE, the Ontario Institute for Studies in Education of the University of

Toronto. For someone who has not grown up in Canada and, for that matter, has completed all his schooling, graduation and post-graduation before coming to Canada, it was an eye opener, a shocker really. I had graduated, done a post graduation, done an additional diploma course, and had not paid thousands of rupees, had never taken a loan to study, nor carried a debt. And, my parents had not had to save for my education from the time I was born. Education in India is, after all, publicly funded. As I went through that course and soaked in hundreds of nitty-gritty details of elementary, secondary, and post-secondary education financing, studied university budgets, financing models, the benefits of education and, of course, the huge *tuition-fee* factor, I saw a new face of life on this side of the Atlantic.

Interestingly enough, as I tried to soak in all those facts, research, and theories, the fascination with this concept never ceased. It gave me some solid facts and reasons to answer the nagging questions in my pre-course naïve mind that asked, "Why was university education in this hemisphere so staggeringly costly?" One of the first lessons learned as parents of a one-year-old starting life in Canada was to "start saving up" for Nathan's education. Obviously, these came from a RESP sales agent who we bumped into at church. We began to educate ourselves on the nuances of the RESP system, the government contribution to match part of our investment, and all those wonderful facts. Strangely enough, it never gave us the peace of mind we would have expected after being so diligent about our son's future education. Like most parents, each year, we routinely got our annual report, showing how many hundreds or thousands of hard earned dollars we had invested, how much of those first hundreds the RESP companies locked away as their own fee, how much the government had chipped in, and the most wonderful projection at the end.

It was this end piece that made you feel like a defeated parent. The report would give a magical year, the year when our son would be going to university, how much it would cost then and, finally, despite everything, how way short we were of that final target. For a middle-income family starting a new life in a new country, then, we knew each dollar that went into that account was slogged for. How did all those thousands of parents that earned salaries barely at the livable level manage? How did those thousands of Canadians that earned those bare minimum salaries of between fifteen and twenty five thousand dollars manage to put away even a penny? According to Ontario's Poverty Reduction report, the target is set on Statistics Canada's low income measure, calculated at 50 percent of the median income. In the city of Toronto, that means a single parent with two kids earning $27,000 a year.

My mind went back to that single parent mentioned at the start of this chapter whose son survived on $750 for meals. How would she ever afford to send him to university if the $750 sufficed for the meals alone? Suddenly, it seemed a little strange. For those who could afford it, whether lavishly or the hard way, or the very hard way, there were additional grants and the millions, nay billions that government invested in post-secondary education.

So, how about those millions that barely lived above or around the poverty line and could never ever save up for their children's education? Wouldn't a university education remain a purely utopian dream for them? Wouldn't it seem a simple answer, education for those who could afford it, with lots of help from the government; and neither post secondary education nor a university or college education for those who could not?

Suddenly, it seemed there were two classes! Class — it's a strange term, littered in history, the epicenter of revolutions, a demarcation of where one group of humans' ends and another begins. Yet, it is simply about the money. If the poor had it then they would study, too, get a higher paying job, and break out of that vicious cycle of poverty.

Again, research tells a great story. Here are a few random tidbits from all the fascinating research and theories that I studied:

- Educational investment automatically generates economic and social benefits to a society.

- Through mandatory education, grants and school subsidies, student scholarships and low-interest loans, making the cost of education tax deductible, and by creating more infrastructure, government can greatly influence the cost side of education.

- Schooling does indeed have a significantly positive effect on income and personal ability determines further education.

- Increase in schooling of the average worker, between 1929 and 1982, explained about one-fourth of the rise in per capita income during this period.

- The key societal benefits of education would be the change in people's perception of themselves and of society around them. Increase in life expectancy, a positive correlation between education and people's ability to adapt to change, and the education of women, results in their joining the workforce and, as a result, a reduction in birth rates.

- Students compelled to complete an extra grade of school have historically experienced an average increase of 9–15% in annual income. Students forced to attend an extra year of school have an average income increase of 12% and better socio-economic outcomes.

- There is a definite causal relationship between educational spending and overall economic growth, with the benefits far exceeding the costs. As a result of investment in public education, personal and corporate incomes increase, which leads to economic development, and this is true for both men and women

- An educated population and workforce lead to fewer social maladies and this in turn encourages economic development and business investment. This in turn directly reduces spending on welfare and on anti-crime programs.

- An educated workforce is also a healthier workforce, thus reducing health care spending.

This would be a long list if one were to try and include every possible research finding. Yet, in plain simple English, we have known for so long that a country's and a society's path to success is through education. Perhaps, the greatest takeaway I had from that course was the concept of human capital Investment in humans that results in an educated population has huge economic benefits and returns. Human beings measured as capital, the value of their skills, the assignment of a monetary value to this, and investment in it to boost productivity, is an old science. One would think that by now our technologically advanced nation would have a super advanced system that could calculate the value of our human capital in real dollar terms. Could you imagine one such high tech computer centre during the recession that hit us in 2008? As hundreds and thousands lost their jobs, the government would actually see a value in each trained professional that hit the road, and plan accordingly. It was the government's billions, after all, that the stimulus spending was using to help turn the economy around.

We could fill our heads with a million facts as to why investment in education works, and still not see the plain simple truth. It is the responsibility of society to provide education or help in its delivery to every single Canadian. Children from poor families are more likely to drop out, and choose work over study. For those aspiring to it, the cost of education may scare them away forever.

I like the term *vicious cycle*, because it represents a pattern that happens over and over again, almost like bondage, in this context. So, if you were poor, you dropped out of school, worked to make ends meet, and, as research tells, filled in the lowest paying jobs, stayed confined to the same socio-economic status, did not have enough to save for your children's education, and then created a new cycle for your children to follow. A sad tradition indeed!

I met a fascinating group of working professionals, at an earlier course at OISE, all from the field of education. We buried ourselves in theories about leading student achievement, educational leadership, the history of education, etc. However, the real truths emerged from group discussions. The solutions seemed so easy: give the students extra help; get the parents over, and help them as well; create study groups; visit them at their homes and convince them to come over; and target the socio-economically challenged, always the group that's challenged in education the most.

That's when I discovered another shocking truth from one teacher's experience. Those same high school students who we thought we could so easily help, academically, worked two or three part time jobs to help their families survive. "Here in Canada?" I gasped, pictures of child labor flashing through my head. After almost nine years in Canada, there was so much more to learn, shamefully. Ok, so get the parents over, I suggested. They were working, as well, evenings and nights.

So, maybe those high school kids could spend their evenings in school, then, I countered. And, this was the final shocker, those high school kids were baby-sitting their younger siblings because the parents were away at work. Suddenly, the picture of a poor slum teen in India, looking after a three-year-old sibling, did not seem so distant.

Oddly enough, or strangely, if one were allowed to put it sarcastically, poverty figures right at the heart of it. Ontario Government's *Breaking the cycle of poverty*, as part of the poverty reduction strategy, has it first chapter dedicated to kids and families and it begins with the lines:

> *The research is clear. Children who grow up in poverty are at a higher risk of living in poverty when they're adults. They're less likely to graduate from high school and less likely to go on to post-secondary education. They're more likely to rely on social assistance as adults and more likely to have children before they are able to support them*[xii].

Aren't these exactly the same people society considers pests? These are the same people who most others wish would get a job and stop living off society and start contributing, always a very vicious cycle.

There is a ton of facts and truths to be found in those few lines, straight from a government document. The federal and provincial governments invest billions in our universities. Today, most would cry about money never being there for elementary and secondary education. We are never satisfied, and after each budget like to complain about its shortcomings. Sadly, yet, the poor student always stands out, despite it all.

Again, there is a ton of research literature on the racial/ethnic minority gap, indicating that substantial achievement gaps remain with long-term economic consequences for low-achieving, minority students. In the US, African American, Hispanic, and high poverty students were 6 to 14.5 months behind in reading and math.

And, finally, to top it off, I learnt of two very enlightening ideologies from the recent past that made me cringe. These two stupid darlings — as I ended up addressing them in my mind, more from my simple sense and not as an insult to those who held that belief — these were the ideologies of *individualism* and *essentialism* and their beliefs about the culture of poverty. While individualism believes it is a personal effort that leads to success, essentialism believes that it is the genetic characteristic that accounts for success or lack thereof. The belief about the culture of poverty proposes that minority groups fail due to the subculture of their homes, communities, and ethnic groups.

I finished my very enlightening course at OISE with a mini research paper entitled, *Government Run Universities: The Case for National Centers of Excellence in Engineering, Medicine and Science in Canada*. India seemed a golden paradise for education and the paper came straight from the heart and less as an academic interest. It was more about writing a research paper that seemed such an apt solution for Canada.

India, a country that in the not too distant past was considered a Third World, underdeveloped, and non-industrialized nation! A nation that was now flooding the world with educated professionals, a country that was now accounting for nearly 40% of the world's software exports, all brain stuff really. Why so, my mind asked? How could a country so classified as poor, Third World, and backward, produce half a million engineers, annually, and an equal number of doctors, and educate whole generations of graduates that could provide a workforce that has driven the country to the heights it is reaching today. That's because it is a country that has invested so heavily in its education. Today, the greatest brain at *Intel*, designing the next generation of processors, could be a product of the famed *Indian Institute of Technology* and would have paid as little as $12 a year for one of the world's best engineering educations!

Is this a proposal to make Canada a fully publicly funded education system? That would take a generation and would be nice. However, this is about Canada taking a small step in helping the best brains as well as the lowest economically placed get a university education. Details of a fully funded university education, one for the brightest minds in the country and another for the most economically challenged in this country are outlined at the end of this chapter. However, here are a few thoughts that make it look quite feasible. It would cost the federal government 0.01% of the total value of the GDP to create a workforce that would be the cream of Canadian intelligence. Where would it take us? To heights unknown and to achievements that would make Canada a world power in leading breakthrough discovery and innovation.

A pleasant discovery really amazed me as I scoured the University of Toronto website looking for details for my paper. My Dad is diabetic. For him and millions like him *insulin* is a daily life-line, without which he would not survive. *Insulin* was discovered here in the research labs of the University of Toronto. Again, it would take 0.01% of the GDP for the federal government to lift thousands of poor Canadians into the world of graduates, a seemingly impossible task today. In a sense, wouldn't that literally break the cycle of poverty? Again, research shows that the poorest kids are most likely to drop out of school and prefer work to education. So, a fully publicly funded federal university for the poorest, with centers all over Canada that provided and cared for all aspects of education, tuition, boarding, and lodging, and produced thousands of graduates, could run on a budget of a billion dollars.

An economist would probably thrash the numbers about federal spending that will be required to sustain two such universities. However, this book is not about technical details. It's about the will to take a step. It's about Canadians, the real forgotten ones, the poor ones, the ones that probably have minds full of intelligence but who, for lack of financial resources, wither into the cycle of poverty that keeps them out of the hallowed institutions of knowledge. It's simply about Canadians helping Canadians.

There is no escaping the simple fact that education requires inputs; it requires funding; it requires targeted funding; and, in brash terms, it requires spending. We could add a ton of theory how that influx of thousands more graduates, engineers, doctors, and of all sorts of university educated professionals, would uplift the economy; or how a huge university educated workforce could change the face of this country, but that is already known. It is known to the academics, known to the businesses that need those graduates, and known to the government that holds the purse strings and the keys to that dream.

Post secondary education or higher education in Canada, as it was known at the start, can be traced back to the early 1800s, to what was then British North America. While they were no match then for the great and antique institutions of Europe, they moved ahead with the spirit enshrined in the words addressed to the then visiting Prince and the future King Edward VII, "Our beginning is but humble – our hopes are in the future". That future is here today and Canadian universities are a testament to that. There can be a new beginning and a new hope for a future that is very near. A future that brings that dream of a university education closer to Canadians that live so far from the dream of ever getting there.

Does the idea of $750 dollars per term, and what it proved, seem so unrealistic now? Maybe not, but there is a lesson there!

A Proposed New Model

While new initiatives and directions and additional funding from all levels of Governments will have to help the current system, this paper proposes two additional models of university education. The two models will target two key segments of students:

- The intellectually brightest students; and,
- The most economically challenged students in Canada.

A. The federal government would

create a "Federal Canadian University for Excellence". This university would have regional centres of learning spread across Canada that will cater to the three key areas of Management, Engineering, and Medicine.

The institutions would offer enrolment to the cleverest minds. Some of the key concepts of such universities would be:

- Fully funded and managed by the federal government
- Enrolment would be open to all Canadians with a small percentage reserved for local (provincial) students
- These institutions would be managed by a National Central Body that would look after syllabus, infrastructure, and all funding needs
- The enrolment numbers would be determined by the National Central Body
- The National Central Body would be responsible for setting and inspecting national standards for these universities
- The provincial governments would be charged a

designated percentage linked directly to the number of students from their province

- Students would pay for entrance exams, forms, transcripts, meals, and text books

- Admission to these centres would be based on
  - o a National entrance/competitive exam based on a pre determined syllabus followed in grades 11 and 12, general Intelligence and IQ tests
  - o actual grades achieved in high school

- These entrance exams would maintain a very rigid standard so as to filter out the most intellectual minds

- Students would be provided education, boarding, and lodging

- They would follow a 4-year graduate program, followed by a Masters, and Doctoral and Research programs

- The Masters, Doctoral, and Research programs would be open to students graduating from all universities across Canada

- These institutes of Management, Medicine, and Technology, would thus create an elite Canadian force of trained professionals

B. The federal government would

create a "Federal Canadian University". This university would have government-funded colleges for the Arts and Sciences that would offer primary enrolment to those defined in the lowest income medians as per Revenue Canada

Some of the key concepts of such universities would be :

- Fully funded and managed by the federal government
- Location and placement of these colleges would be based on concentration and distribution of the local population
- Enrolment would be provided primarily to the provincial population (starting with the lowest income levels)
- These institutions would be managed by a National Central Body that would look after syllabus, infrastructure, and all funding needs
- The enrolment numbers would be determined by the National Central Body
- The National Central Body would be responsible for setting and inspecting national standards for these colleges
- The provincial governments would share an equal percentage of the costs
- Students would pay for forms, transcripts, meals, and text books
- Admission to these colleges would be based on
    - Lowest income levels
    - Completion of high school
- Students would be provided education, boarding, and lodging
- They would follow a 3-year graduate program
- The syllabus would reflect a wide variety and scope of

courses relevant to the local and evolving needs

- These institutes would help those that severely lack the financial means to get admission to a college and university

- These institutes would have to follow strict performance standards, with students and the college itself having to perform at acceptable standards as determined by the central governing body.

Why, and what would these achieve?

- The federal government currently bears no direct mandated responsibility for university and post-secondary education.

- As discussed earlier in the paper, post-secondary education can become a victim of economic circumstances, party manifestos and the rulings of different political parties in power. The fact that a federal government could with impunity withdraw a sizeable chunk of federal funding and leave universities and students to come up with the necessary funds by way of increased tuitions fees is an example of this.

- In taking responsibility for these institutions, the government would have to undertake its responsibility directly and not on an ad hoc basis.

- On a national scale, this would also create a central system that would regulate opportunities for students across Canada regardless of their own economic status or that of their provinces.

- Intellectual capacity and achievement would be the only determining factors in this quest.

- Nationally, it would also drive student achievement and learning on a designated path, first to achieve the required level through competition, as well as to maintain a level of consistency and achievement through high school.

- For the economically challenged, it would provide an incentive to complete high school and be assured of a realistic chance of a university education

- Additionally, it would create a sense of fairness, so that no deserving mind would be barred access to learning due to economic shortcomings.

- Accountability would a key benefit with these universities and colleges, being directly controlled by their sources of funding

- The provincial involvement in both types of institutions would mandate a certain level of commitment from the provincial government

- Creation of these institutes would directly challenge existing institutions to remain competitive by way of facilities, staff salaries, and programs offered

- The federal government through these institutions could directly answer the shortages of medical doctors, engineers, research scientists, and other valued professional, rather than having to rely on immigration.

- These institutions would create state-of-the-art laboratories, libraries, and research facilities that would benefit the nation as a whole

- A source of pride for the nation. As these institutions excel, flourish, produce technical advancement, innovation and ground-breaking research, they will attract the best and brightest talent from around the world

- Institutions for the economically challenged will be a huge factor in breaking the cycle of poverty that would for generations keep these people out of higher and post-secondary education. It will directly force both levels of government to invest in the poor by way of dedicated budgets to these institutions.

Conclusion

This little section highlights the possibilities of what can be achieved through publicly funded university education. For Canada to provide direct and targeted funding for a limited number is a real possibility. With a majority of the rich and the middle class already benefiting from government spending in part towards their university education, the government would answer the call of society, industry, and the economy at large, by making real the possibility of a targeted publicly funded post-secondary education. It would ensure that the poorest sections graduate with no debt at all and remove the barrier of an economic hurdle from the path of the best intellectuals. Inadvertently, it would draw together the finest intellectual talent into closer proximity and further the cause and quality of research and development

Youth and Crime 111

Youth and Crime

On November 14, 2008, a report was

released named *Roots of Youth Violence*[xiii]. The report, running into hundreds of pages, identified a number of causes of youth violence in our society. These included poverty, racism, culturally insensitive education systems, and limited job prospects. The odd part, the report was released exactly three days after a stabbing at the same school where a year ago a 15-year-old named Jordan Manners had been shot, on school property. The report was commissioned because of the shooting of Jordan Manners. It identified factors such as low self-esteem, alienation, and hopelessness, as the results of the various causes identified above that were responsible for spiraling youth violence. A highlight of the violence: guns. The report said that, as more and more violent cases were being reported, the use of guns, specifically hand- guns, was increasing.

Have you ever held a gun? If not, then assume for a minute that you have! And then picture yourself after a James Bond movie, or a western, or a ton of action films. Picture yourself standing in front of your mirror, walking in like Bond does in that famous red circle. Would you not imitate the classic Bond move and turn and shoot into the mirror? How many times have you held an object that even remotely resembled a gun and, before you knew it, you were 007, or a gun-blazing *Billy the Kid*, or one of so many others plentifully found in the movies?

At what age do we discover guns? Isn't that the taboo word we so skillfully censor out of our talk as our kids grow? We spell it out, hit the mute button faster than the censors with their bleeps, as we see it day after day on the news, so careful to protect our innocent little ones from the mere mention of that word. It does not last long, as you discover your four- or five-year-old spelling it back to you. Of course they know it, even better than us, from all the television they watch. Light sabers, laser guns, paint ball guns, water guns, and the actual dart shooting ones, a fancy new product called *Nerf*. If you were to *Google* the word *Nerf*, through the *Websense* filter of a school board, you would hit the stop screen in a millisecond. Wonder why? Go to the *Toys R Us* website and look up the same word. The range of products will fascinate you, whether you like guns or not. Like automatic guns, the description boasts of the rapid fire of darts, probably eight in a row. So, to keep it going, you could buy a whole magazine, probably a 25-pack refill conveniently mounted on an ammo belt. Does your kid own one? There are so many of them that own one, the almost real looking ones, even if they are crude toys from the dollar store.

Even if you consciously have not bought one for your kid, it's only a matter of time before one makes its way into their world, at a friend's place, a park, or "anywhere kids may be found". How it captures their imagination is unknown, but it is almost like love at first sight. If you were to capture their make believe games, each with a gun in hand, complete with the falls, rolls, and super marksmanship, and the sounds to match, I'm sure you would have a few very good Bond moves ready for the next movie.

So, what do you expect of kids, living on the streets, dealing with drugs, gangs, and violence, from a tender age? These are the poor kids, financially poor, especially the ones that grow up in crime-ridden neighborhoods. The ones who grow up so fast, always by default on the wrong side of the law, grow into perfect misfits of society. Perfectly cast out, with no education, no money and, of course, all the time on the street. Does it not sound like a classic social theory or a typical sociology lesson taught a million times in our universities? A poor kid, shut out of society, despised, hungry, poor, looking out to a world full of glamour and wealth. Does he see the church and the school around the corner? Or does he see the dealer around the corner, with the flashy cars, designer clothes, and the huge cash flow?

Picture another scene. It's Boxing Day, December 26, 2005, on Yonge Street, Toronto, packed with shoppers. It is the festive season and, of course, a day of bargains, a day when North Americans spend billions on the special deals available. It was also the day when two gangs of youth decided to kick off a shooting spree, right in the middle of the street. Not one of the gang members was injured, except for a lot of innocent bystanders. Tragically, Jane Creba a 15-year-old grade 10 student, shopping with her sister, caught one of the stray bullets and died. A happy 15-year-old with no connection to the crime or to the gang of 10 or 15 that shot at each other in the middle of that crowd. A 15-year-old with the smile of an angel, a love of green apples, and a future full of promise!

How much do you think has changed from 2005, in the four or five years since then? Ask Clemee Joseph, mother of 18-year-old Jarvis St. Remy, as she buried him, a week before Mother's day, in May 2009 and a month before his graduation. An 18-year-old with no connection to drugs, crime, and no criminal history. Just a black youth, mistakenly shot at a bus stop.

So, whose responsibility is it? Really, blame it on poverty! Or blame it on the drug dealers! Or blame it on guns and the lifestyle of these youth! Or simply just blame it on their background, the apathy of their parents, and a host of factors. Blame it on the city, a municipal problem, where the mayor has been crying his lungs out for a ban on hand guns. Blame it on the province, for not providing enough to keep them in education. Blame it on the federal government, for not getting rid of that irritating nuisance called poverty, or for not creating enough laws regarding hand guns, or for not creating opportunities for these youth.

Sadly, the deaths of two teens, or the countless others not listed here, were not enough for any drastic plan of action that had this issue as its primary focus. What is it that is lacking in our society, or in our leaders, that allows them to see such incident after incident and still carry on? The reports come, months later, some laws, some more funds, and maybe some more committee meetings, some weekend activities, and end of story. It's the same half baked effort that goes on and on year after year, so grossly inadequate that for every youth that it tries to save, another hundred enter the horrendous world of crime. The federal Conservative government that came into power after the Jane Creba shooting brought stricter legislation and threatened some real serious ones but, in the next election, they lost the majority they thought was surely theirs for the taking. Why? One of the reasons — the same stiffer sentences they proposed on these youth.

So, if you can digest this, here is the last factual piece on the same shootings in the same city, Toronto. In the same year that Jane Creba was shot, the city of Toronto had 80 homicides recorded and 52 shooting deaths, a record for the city. A mere month before that, on November 18, 2005, a youth named Amon Beckles was killed at a funeral, horrifically, outside a church. Even more tragically, this was a funeral for another youth, Jamal Hemmings, who was also a victim of a shooting. What was Amon's fault? He may have witnessed Jamal's shooting death. Do you happen to find a strange connection between youth, crime, guns, and shooting? In all, 10 persons were arrested, of whom three happened to be youth. Andre Thompson, 20, one of the accused, was out on probation. Another 17-year-old remained unidentified, protected by the *Youth Criminal Justice Act*. Of those charged with second degree murder, one was 19 and another 24. One of those charged in the shooting, Eric Boateng, was shot dead in another incident. Sad!

Those of us who lived through those events may have recoiled in horror as each one unfolded. Sure, we may not admit it openly, but for sure, we would have looked at a particular segment of society and felt good on our little sanctified pedestals. We may have even felt good about how we were not part of the problem. I'm sure some of us may have even condemned every single one of those involved in these events. After all, those who live by the sword die by the sword, or so we would have thought.

We read these details, facts, year after year. The same incidents get reported year after year. The same politicians, city councilors, provincial MPPs, and federal MPs stand for elections during these same periods, and get elected and reelected, year after year. And yet, do you see a single large concerted project that targets this problem? Torontonians faithfully elect, and re-elect, and re-elect, and re-elect, and then again re-elect some of the same twenty-odd members of parliament, term after term. Yet, after having such a strong presence in Ottawa, how many projects do you see that go after youth crime in Toronto? Do you see a large banner across the city, on the TTC, across every news publication that says, "We will fix it"? Do you see a single individual with a single vision of fixing it? Do you see anything that says this is an all out war on crime, on youth poverty, on youth alienation, on youth illiteracy, and on so many social issues? If a bunch of Councilors, MPPs, MPs, social workers, and law agencies, attacked this issue, single-mindedly, would there be a change in the social scene? You bet there would be. Again, looking at the Toronto scene and knowing that this was very much a black youth issue, what if someone roped in a bunch of *NBA* stars, or the *Raptors*, and maybe a Will Smith, or a local version of the Rev Jesse Jackson? And, what if those bunch of Toronto MPs, (and there is a whole lot of them from Toronto), got together and made sure a few hundred thousands were available to relocate these youth, and get them into educational and counseling programs? And, what if, knowing that the might of society was behind such a project, law agencies were given a chance to go into these very specific known areas with an increased presence and build bridges with these communities, so that there would be no place left for the drug dealers, the gun dealers, and the harbingers of death?

So, what do we lack? A social will to deal with these problems, or a political will to deal with these problems, or even a religious will to deal with these problems? The vast majority of Canadians still identify themselves as belonging to a religion. What if every single church and religious institution joined hands with the local, provincial, and federal government, and reached out to these youth and their families? Would we have turned over a sad page? Yes! I say yes, it is possible. All it takes is one man's vision to lead the way. One man with convictions, and the desire to fix it, would fix it; someone with a vision or someone radical enough to break convention.

Remember Mayor Frank Melton, from Mississippi. The man with the catchphrase, "And that, my friends, is the bottom line". A mayor who walked the poor neighborhoods, dared to lecture youth about hard work and accountability, tried brokering peace among gangs and could still be tough on crime. Would we have a utopia after that? No, crime would still find its way onto our streets. But isn't that what it is, a constant battle between good and evil? But here it would be a battle where good would constantly be beating the evil and the little sparks of evil that would fly from time to time would easily be snuffed out.

What would I do if I were Prime Minister, or the Premier, or even an MP or an MPP of this city? I would stake my career on this one problem. I would start a movement, given my social standing, and the power and the resources placed in my hands by the people. Day after day, week after week, I would pull in every single body that was morally obliged to take its share of the responsibility and make them work for it. For, if for one term I was able to do something on this one issue, I would know I had achieved more than the many hours spent in comfy leather chairs in the hallowed halls of the legislatures and city halls. Is there someone listening or reading that fits the bill and is willing to take responsibility, before a few more innocent Jane Crebas are shot?

What could be the answer to what may seem like a cry for help? How about if we sentenced these youth to special prisons that looked like little homes behind bars, where they lived in little teams, classified according to their IQ, aptitudes, and interests, with endless sentences where the only way out was earned by achievement in education, in learning a trade, completing their incomplete education, maybe online, good behavior, and recovering and rediscovering a part of their lost childhood and teen years? What if we then made them work their way out, through half-way homes that were real homes, where they lived, worked, earned, and learned to save, under supervision. And, then, as they made their way out of these places, well-funded programs helped them settle into new lives, into jobs that did not just give them money but actually helped them give back to society.

Can we recreate, rebuild these lost lives? How many times do we read that prison makes them better criminals rather than better citizens? Do the ones that go there, for the first time, come out emboldened and recruited? Do they find links to gangs that exist there, or simply learn new tricks? If one were to justify it, would it cost us more, financially and morally, to help these kids with genuine reformation homes and programs, or would it cost us more to keep throwing them back into filthy prisons that would turn out to be refresher courses and crime addiction fixes for their destroyed lives? There is a ton of research for these kinds of programs. A million innovative programs have been tried and tested, and so many of these have worked.

I once read of a program in the US that sent kids who had taken their first steps into crime to spend a few hours with the most hardened criminals. If the criminals managed to scare the kids away from crime, or literally scared the hell out of them with the actual sight of what their future looked like, the criminals earned a few good luxuries, and the kids learned a good reason to stay away from crime. Cities and provinces, or governments, on their own, cannot fix it. A concerted action that lets the experts, those that work and specialize in this, the social workers, the law enforcers, and the ones who want to fix it, let them fix it. Let the others help with resources, funding, and jobs. Then, step in and create an environment that helps these kids step away from crime. From the 1908 *Youth Juvenile Delinquents Ac*t, to the *Young Offenders Act* of 1982 to the *Youth Criminal Justice Act* of 2007, we have had Parliament do its share of legislation and ruling. Does it work? Yes, it does, and sets the ground and the framework for how we deal with our juvenile youth.

However, we still debate, politically, who is tough on crime, based on our ideology. So, what do we do with the 17-year-old that carries a hand gun and, not mercilessly, but without a care, guns down another 17-year-old? That's where we go grey. We fight to sentence them as adults, and then debate endlessly over the justice meted out to these youth.

I end this chapter with one last thought. Statistics are great, and helpful. Our lives are now built around data, past and current data that even projects the future. So, what does it say about crime? In Toronto, for example, we proudly claim that the crime rate is still lower than similar sized American cities. As for the rest of Canada, we are on par with other Canadian cities. Should we then conclude that the 80 odd homicides, including the one of Jane Creba, were ok or acceptable, they after all were a stat lower than the US and the same as the rest of Canada?

How can we live with the fact that in the same city, where one corner of the city boasts of arts, theatre, culture, high social life, and wealth, another poor quarter lives with drugs, violence, and death, dealt by youth. Sure, it is not a unique problem. It exists all over the world, but is that our excuse? Detective Sergeant Kyriacou of the Toronto Police said this of the Jane Creba shooting, "Toronto has finally lost its innocence". Did we realize it then or did we know that we had lost our innocence a long time ago? Did it take the death of an innocent sweet girl to melt our hearts, even if for a few seconds, to realize this? So, do we want to do something about it, or do we want to live with it, till maybe another Jarvis St. Remy gets gunned down or may be a stray bullet catches the mayor or the daughter of the billionaire who just donated a million dollar piece of art to the *Art Gallery of Ontario*? Is that when we will wake up?

Check out the Roots of Youth Violence report at this address:

http://www.rootsofyouthviolence.on.ca/english/index.asp

Fat Kids or Gold Medallists   123

Fat Kids or Gold Medallists

My Dad and I have this phone

conversation every winter a few times, he in India and I from here in Canada. Our conversation begins with the usual pleasantries, news, and relatives, till it invariably gets to the weather. For some vague reason, I find myself bragging to him of all the things that a Canadian would never brag about. I'm referring to the white stuff as we sometimes call it or, by whatever other name, just plain snow. It totally changes our lives for the months that it is with us — the sub zero temperatures, the tons of snow on the ground, the wind chills, the blizzards, the treacherous driving conditions, etc. It's good old man winter, we say, even when it chills us down to our bones, makes us wear layers of clothing, adjust our driving habits, put away the barbecue, and say good bye to the backyard. To someone listening in to that conversation it would almost sound as if I was trying to make my Dad jealous. "Where are the kids?" he invariably asks me. "Outside, playing in the snow", I tell him, more bragging, as if they were out rolling on a chocolate and marshmallow dream beach. After an eternity of lectures and arguments, my stance moves from my super hero sons (for playing in the snow) to the downright truth. "Daddy, they need to get out; they need the fresh air; they need the physical activity and the fun; or else they won't grow. Besides, they love it".

Try and remember the scene on a typical weekend or

holiday when you peep outside in the winter. There is snow everywhere, beautiful white snow; it's everywhere, on the trees, on the cars, even inside the cars, on the shrubs, on the grass and the rooftops. Other than the odd bundled up figure rushing home, it's almost like a Hollywood thriller, the deserted landscape with the lone figure waiting to get home before the attack of the aliens, or may be like a horror movie, before the evil fog sets in. I make it sound exaggeratedly bleak but, really, where are the kids? Where are the hundreds and thousands of them?

According to *Statistics Canada*, over 5.2 million kids attend our elementary and secondary schools. Of these, Ontario alone had over two million in 2008. Where are they in the winter when not in school? Sure, a lot of enterprising moms and dads, with their little extra or hard-earned budgeted dollars, have them into some form of swimming, karate, hockey, and various other programs. Some may be off skiing or various other winter sports. Many would be in some form of city-run program. What percentage is that of the total number of kids out there?

In the 2008 Beijing Summer Olympics, Canada had the 8th largest delegation with 332 athletes. Our whole country watched them leave with great hopes; we wished them well and then sat and waited for the medals to roll in. When did the medals start rolling in? Was it on the first day, second day, third day, maybe the fourth or fifth day? Not on any of them. If you followed the press and the various news reports, you would have heard the gradual din of protests and mumbles grow as we saw country after country, small and big, some poor, some underdeveloped, countries of all types take home the medals. Past athletes and sports officials were quick to point out that Canada traditionally did not start winning till the second week. If you looked at the medals tally on Day 7, it featured countries like Cuba, Azerbaijan, Slovakia, and even an impoverished and destroyed country like Zimbabwe. Cuba had six medals by then and Zimbabwe not one but three silvers. At the top end of the table, China had 22 gold medals and the US and China between them had 70 medals.

Let's jump back to the *People for Education: Annual Report on Ontario's School 2008*[xiv]. As per the report, Canadian children and youth get a failing grade in their level of physical activity, according to *Active Healthy Kids Canada*. The report further states that only 44% of elementary schools in Ontario had a physical education teacher, while the Ontario education policy required physical education classes from kindergarten to grade 9.

A growing body of research illustrates that exercise can boost the brain power in children and adolescents. Harvard university professor Dr. John J. Rately states, "The exercise itself doesn't make you smarter, but it puts the brain of learners in the optimal position for them to learn".[15]

What does it really mean? There is a future Olympian, many future Olympians, who can bring home the medals that are sitting in our classrooms. Closer to the basics, there are millions of kids in our schools that need to get up and get out for their hour of physical education. There are millions of them who, if given a chance and the opportunity to step out on a track, would have taken their first steps into a healthy, athletic world. There are hundreds of future medal holders sitting in our homes through the long winters, with their *Sony PS3s*, their *XBox 360s*, or with their *Wii*s, achieving nothing. We're proud of it, proud of ourselves that we can get them all those costly gizmos; we're rich after all, advanced. So where do we start? Is it all about the medals? Is it about the winning, the gold, the silver, and the bronze, and how many medals we bring home?

"*Citius, Altius, Fortius*", or "*Faster, Higher, Stronger*", goes the motto of the Olympics. It's not about that big event that happens every four years, but it's about a sense of achievement, a sense of purpose, and a sense of ambition that can drive our youth to that goal. It's about the youth of this country, on the move, alive, active, and moving with a sense of purpose. It's about the youth of this country, fired up; fired up to take on their lives with a sense of purpose. It's about plain healthy kids with healthy habits, the future of our country.

Let's jump back to those snowy days. I've been home with my kids through *March Break*, sometimes the few extra days before Christmas, or maybe the few PA days. I have stood and watched in frustration as the only options for the day would be a movie, the mall, *Chuck e Cheese*'s, *McDonald*'s or *Wendy*'s, for a while a roll in the snow or a toboggan ride down a nearby slope. I once asked my Grade 8 Confirmation class to rate their level of fun and excitement at the end of their *March Break*. Before I could put out a scale of my well thought out 1 to 10 with 1 being the *blah blah* I heard myself saying, all ten of them had already yelled out, "Boring". Suddenly, it struck me that between me, the school, the parish, the parents, and so many others who could have been involved, these young teens had spent 10 long days doing nothing.

Does it frustrate you that with all our wealth and resources, our abundance of food, our general state of richness and good health, we don't have the facilities where we could take our kids to let them run on a track, or jump in a sand pit, or do a high jump. Doesn't it seem so ridiculously obvious that we could have massive programs of coaches and camps, where we could have the youth of this country, first and foremost, healthy and active, not just in the summer, but throughout the year, even on the coldest snowy days?

I know by now that many of you would be having your guard up, thinking of the Soviets, the Chinese, and some other state-run programs where the sense of purpose, the sense of sports, the sense and the spirit of the Olympics was lost, where it became nothing more than a state machine that mechanically produced those champions, as another victory over the West. We could find that and hundreds of other reasons to justify not doing it.

So who are these few athletes who bring home the medals? In a country where abundance, surpluses, big energy corporations, oil companies, and the super rich banks, and many other such things are realities, how much would it take to get a country on the move? How much would it take to get a nation massively involved, not in a mechanically Communist way, but in a way only we Canadians can do — Through our passion, through our goodness, through our sense of involvement, through our community spirit, and through our sense of victory which has brought us to the economic state we are at?

On Day 8 of the Beijing Olympics, wrestler Carol Huynh of Hazelton, B.C., won Canada's first gold medal. The 27-year-old captured gold in the 48-kilogram freestyle over Japan's Chiharu Icho. As Carol stood singing *O Canada* on the podium, she cried. Commenting on her reaction later she said, "I was just thinking how proud I am to be Canadian, and I was just thinking about the road how I got here. It's been a long but good one". Carol is the daughter of Vietnamese immigrants and she thanked the people of Hazelton for their support and help in raising an Olympian.

The Huynhs came to Canada as refugees, known as the boat people. More than a million of them fled their homes in the Indochinese homelands after the Vietnam War in barely seaworthy vessels. Of the million that escaped, Canada accepted 60,000, and more than half this number were sponsored by private citizens or, as in the case of the Huynhs, by church groups. The United Church congregation built them a small home, more of a barn built by the men around. The family knew just two words, *Hi* and *Thank you*. The generosity of the Church helped this little family begin their Canadian journey. And what did that victory do for this little town? I quote you these lines from *The Globe and the Mail*, August 18, 2008:

> *In Hazelton and its surrounding hamlets and reserves, the chance to support an aspiring athlete brought together communities for whom economic deprivation is common, and tragedy only too familiar. The hardships have been ignored, even if only temporarily, as they have cheered on one of their own doing battle half a world away.*

How do you think it inspired those people to see Carol, one of their own, conquer the world that day?

The story of Carol Huynh has so many basics to learn from. Here is another little piece from that article in *The Globe and Mail*:

> *Joe Sullivan, a burly, barrel-chested military veteran, inherited the Hazelton Secondary wrestling program when he moved to the village in 1986. He had an open-door policy. Any student – fat or skinny, clumsy or agile – could join the wrestling team. At one point, he had 50 members, one-10th of the school population. He designed the workouts to be as much a social event as physical exercise. He also combined fundraising with fitness training and bought a wood splitter and chainsaws, as well as an old truck for deliveries, so the team could cut and sell firewood.*

In our cities and metros, how many Joe Sullivans do we need? If that little village could have one tenth of its kids in an open program, with all our resources, how many kids could we have in similar programs and how many Carols would be produce?

So how many people did it take to raise an Olympian? How many Canadians did that moment inspire? Not to become Olympians and win gold; maybe that, but the millions it inspired to first feel that great Canadian feel, of belonging, of winning, and then to step up and step on in the things they did in their daily lives. If a community like Hazelton, with its economic hardships, with suicide among its youth a real concern, could pull together, what could be a more glowing example for the rest of Canada?

Do you remember Daniel Igali, the freestyle wrestler who won gold for Canada in the 2000 Sydney Olympics? What is fantastic about Igali is that this wrestler came from a poor little village in Nigeria. "People from the village don't go to the Olympics", his village teacher once told him, "Don't waste your time dreaming about things you can't achieve". It was plain talk about the reality facing this young kid. That kid didn't just make it to the Olympics but made it all the way to the gold.

Sportsmen and sportswomen always inspire us in many ways but it's the little snippets from special moments in their lives that leave a lasting impression on us. Those are the impressions that inspire not just their own countries, but all men and women for generations. When Igali won his medal, he wore the Canadian flag like a cape, was almost swallowed in it. He then took it off, carefully placed it on the mat, and then knelt down and kissed it. How many generations will that inspire or what higher honor could you have seen accorded to the Canadian flag in a long time? If these little communities could get together and help a single person rise to stardom, to conquer, to bring together a nation, then do we even need to look for huge solutions? How many millions or how few millions would it need for a country like ours to make sports a part and parcel of our lives? How many governments would it take to make sports a central part of our lives? How many huge corporations would it take to put together a few millions, probably a fraction of the bonuses taken home by those top executives, to create an Olympian?

These verses are not about the solutions. We have them aplenty. It would not take us more than a few years to put together massive well-funded programs that would give us our results. It takes one government to start the process. It takes one minister, or prime minister, to stand in one large field with a few thousand Olympians to let them know that their quest is not just their own personal quest through hard raised dollars and a life of struggle, no matter what the glory they brought or not for their country.

It's surprising how the word poverty seems to crop up even when we talk about sports. Sure, we don't have it in ice hockey, or basketball, or baseball, we don't mind them earning millions. Yet, how many people would you find in Asia or, more specifically, in India, China, and Australia, three massive sporting nations, that know the name, Matt Sundin? Let's remember another great athlete, Gary Reed. Gary won a lot of medals in the Olympics and the World championship events but missed the bronze in a tough race at Beijing. I remember watching an interview of his and, even though I don't have a written quote or a recorded interview, the one time he said this stuck in my mind forever. "I know what it means to have nothing", were Gary's words. When he referred to nothing, he meant absolutely nothing, as in an empty dinner table.

That's the kind of spirit that we need to inspire our youth. That's the kind of spirit that can take our kids from their couches and gaming consoles to the heights of human excellence. It would not matter how many hundreds made it to the Olympics and even fewer to the podiums. The millions that would end up picking up their lives, their love of their country, a habit of success, and a sense of hard work — that would be irreplaceable. It would produce generations of achievers that would take this great country of ours from the good to the great.

After the Beijing Olympics, the Harper Government wanted to reward the medal winners with cash. I thought, finally a just monetary reward for these hardworking sportsmen and sportswomen. You'd think the public would back it wholeheartedly, that these men and women who brought us glory on the world stage, who put our name right up there in the list of champions, would take home a fortune? You'd think they got something big enough to compensate them for every time the medal count was looked at, their gift to their nation would be recognized. You'd think that for these young men and women, having given away the best years of their life to achieving glory for the country, there would be enough compensation not to have to worry about planning for their future, after their youth was over.

I am not sure if I would dare to mention the measly amount or painfully quote you line after line from news analyses that debated the very act of cash rewards for our athletes. So typical of so many other issues, we forgot the act and practiced our intelligence in hair splitting social issues surrounding the act. Why not a million dollars for Gold, $500,000 for Silver, $250,000 for Bronze, $100,000 for qualifying, and a big thank you for daring to achieve and earn glory for the country?

While we may debate this and other such measures, we need to get back to the basics. For years, the government has cut funding for sports. A single government that is *for* the people could reverse those cuts and kick start our Olympic quest, not just for the medals, but for a nation that would come together like the little town of Hazelton that showed how Canadians for Canadians can achieve more than any book could. How much does our government chip in? $40 million maybe? However, it's not just about what the government puts in? It's also about how much a government can mobilize for our athletes. Do the athletes need to go begging, literally, to the big corporate sponsors to raise money for their survival and their costly equipment? Does it have to be a choice between survival, practice, and fund raising?

There is a way, there are thousands of ways where we could have world class athletes, trained in world class centers, all across Canada, supported by a miniscule fraction of the profits from the corporate world.

So, who made the rule or the tradition that we would only start winning from the 8th day? Or, who made the rule that the sports of the first few days were not our strengths? Or, who made the rule that trying to get into the top 20 was grand? There are no limitations or boundaries for what we can achieve as Canadians. We just have not done it or dared to dream beyond where we are.

So, going back to our long winter months, do we need massive indoor stadiums worth hundreds of millions of dollars? Do we need to kick the *Blue Jays* out of the *Rogers Centre* and send in the army to capture it for our kids to have a ground to use all through the winter? I used to think so, till an invitation to an IT conference with a chance to swing away at a bucket full of golf balls in early spring caught my attention. I am not a golfer, but once a year I faithfully spend the day on the golf course as an attendee at the *ECNO Conference,* when I attend it. The first target is to actually connect the swing with that little ball on the tee and not have my hand vibrate like the Big Ben from the impact of smacking my club into the green. And, then, if I could get it past the marker for the ladies tee off, I would come away with my head held high. So, at the end of winter of 2009, when the invitation came to join in a quick IT discussion about emerging server technologies and the new *Intel Nehalem* chip, followed by an hour swinging away at golf balls, I promptly signed up. Given the season, I reached there expecting an apology for a cancellation due to the rainy or soggy conditions. And, then, thinking I was horribly lost looking for a golf course in the middle of an industrial estate, a huge white bubble of a golf dome clicked endless answers in my head. Suddenly, that cloudy spring day took the cloud from my mind. Here, in front of me, stood a solution that spelt not one massive stadium worth hundreds of millions of dollars in one city, but sports centers in towns and cities for hundreds of thousands of kids. As always, something in my mind said, "No massive costly solutions needed here, but simple solutions, that someone could dare to pay attention to" — simple solutions, with a dedicated vision and facilities and support given to hundreds of Joe Sullivans across the nation. The winter calendar would be so busy with track and field, gymnastics, swimming, diving, and any number of physical sports, that parents would be busy getting their super fit competing kids into competitions across the country, rather than looking for costly getaways in the winter to the sunny south, or more games for those gaming consoles. What would our kids dream of? Would they dream of competing, first and foremost, in local events, and then provincially and nationally? Would they dream of running the fastest, or jumping the highest, in their schools, and then nationally, and then being the fastest in the world? Would they dream of being athletes throughout the year, as part of their curriculum, of being healthy, and then having the assurance that this rich nation could afford and provide a lot more than it does today? What effect would it have on their general lives? It would be a humongous one, in terms of achievement that extends to all walks of life, starting with academics.

As we went through those Beijing Olympics, day after day, I gave my sons all the time in front of the television, a rarity, hoping that some athlete there would light a spark in them. "Wouldn't you like to do that huge Flosbury-flop?" I asked my ten- and six-year-old sons, or do that triple jump or throw a discus or a shot-putt? It was all Greek to them.

It took me back to one of the most remarkable days on any school calendar in India, the Sports Day. It was like a mini Olympics day at school. We prepared for it for weeks; the heats and the qualifying rounds that would start well in advance, and then would come the big day — the finals, the colorful march past, and finally the awesome drill display put up by everyone from Grade 1 to 10. It was all an unknown concept to my son and I had to accept the fact that hundreds of thousands of kids in Canada would complete schooling without ever holding a discus, a shot putt, or a javelin. They would never ever try to do a high jump, or a long jump, or a triple jump. Most of all, they would never know what an endless world of opportunities and achievement existed right through their growing years.

A glorious healthy Olympic dream and the thoughts of being high on that table of medals would be a sweet dream and a nice way of ending this chapter. A Canada that becomes a super power at the Olympics, the thoughts that the Canadians were going to the Olympics to sweep the medals in the pool, a Canadian Michael Phelps, and Canadians who were now challenging the Americans and the Chinese for the top spots on the medal table, all would be a great future to dream of. We would be a country full of past, present, and future Olympians, who had all competed at being the best in the world, and then carried that spirit into all walks of life. A Canada where athletes did not have to divide their time between achieving their best now and worrying for the future, but worked hard, content that they could devote their energies and talents to the sport, and the rest would be taken care of. That's a dream far away though, and the stories of under funded athletes abound in plenty. Ask boxer Adam Trupish who went to the 2008 Olympics with just one support staff person, a coach, manager, physiotherapist and psychologist all rolled in one. How did he finance himself? He worked well into the final stages rather than practice and, of course, a $25,000 dollar personal debt. However, a quote, raw and angry, from one of those famous follow up responses to the many online articles is what really got me on this thought. However partial, biased, myopic, and subjective a view the thought may be, it is a good reflection of what the world of our athletes may be like:

> Posted 2008/12/18 at 9:54 AM ET:
>
> Here's the truth if you can handle it. In 2004, 2 of my athletes made it to the Olympics in sport we hadn't qualified in as a team since the 70's. You know how many times TSN, CBC or any other company gave these kids any coverage prior to the games? Once. One measly time. Let me give you a snapshot.
>
> - 2 girls under 18, both had to move away from their families, go to another school, train 20-24 hours per week minimum.
>
> - You know how much money they got from the government? Less than the poverty level.
>
> -Other funding? NONE. Not a dime.
>
> -Coaches? Some paid their own way to go.

-You know what they did get? A cell phone, some clothes, some toiletries.

-You know when they left? Early June to train in Europe

-Where are they now? In another country with full blown scholarships because they actually appreciate the talent, both have had surgery because they trained so hard to represent their country at any cost. They gave up their family, their friends, more than any of us under 18 ever had to. We expect these CHILDREN to perform at their best, tear up their bodies for really, nothing. Unless they want an education paid for oh and guess what, they have to leave the country again for that. And for a country that really, doesn't appreciate it.

The next time someone wants to say how crappy our athletes are and that they are drunks and mediocre, come with me to work, say it to their face. Ya, it sucks they have the talent and unfortunately grow up in a place that doesn't support them. They'll tell you their sorry they tried their best, practice for 4 hours, then go back to an empty apartment they live in because they can't live with their family.

To Green Gold 139

To Green Gold

A few murders, assassinations,

gruesome torture, including water boarding, prison riots and escapes, the electric chair, and a few nail biting twists and turns finally led to the UN obtaining Scylla. Michael Scofield and Lincoln Burrows, along with Sarah Tancredi, and the rest of the gang, were finally pardoned and given a clean slate. The General? Well, he finally got just what he deserved, the electric chair.

Sounds like an international incident that you swear you could not have missed. No, this is not from real life. And what is Scylla anyway? If you followed the TV series *Prison Break*, you would remember waiting for that once a week hour, where you sat on the edge of your couch wondering who'd die next and how unexpectedly the plot would twist. Through the many escapes of Scofield and Burrows, from the many jails, you would know the many countless plots, murders, assassinations, and the actual escapes of the two innocent brothers along with a band of ruthless thugs. The whole series, which gripped audiences for a few years, follows the trail of a ruthless company and the efforts of the various secret organizations in trying to obtain Scylla. Ultimately, what was thought to be a secret black book that could bring down the all-powerful company turns out to be a lot more. Scylla, a data card, closely guarded by virtually impregnable security systems, agents that kill on a whim, and the final access to it obtainable only through six secret data cards carried by six different top company heads which when put through a special decoder, together, reveal the data inside it. It involved national governments, homeland security, assassination of the Indian Prime Minister's son and finally the UN. Scylla, the little data card, contained a revolutionary theory on alternate forms of energy — a theory so revolutionary that it could change the face of the earth. From new forms of capturing solar energy to generating unlimited power for good and bad. It touched everything from nuclear, wind, fuel, water, medicine, and crops, to *bargain*. *Bargain*, a company-derived acronym for the four periodic elements Boron, Argon, Gallium and Indium. These four elements, when combined with solar power, could create unlimited renewable energy. It could also create super powerful bombs, both conventional and chemical. There was even a solar cell prototype, a desalination technique to yield potable water in seconds, futuristic vaccines, and super yielding bio-engineered crop technology. Wow to Hollywood for that, always ahead of the real world! If Scylla really existed, we would have turned over a new chapter in the history of humanity and we would not be here worrying about our planet.

It may have been in grade 4 or 5, we may not remember, but from those years in school we all learnt one basic law of science that none of us will ever forget, "Energy cannot be created or destroyed". Remember the famous pendulum experiment or whatever memory you have of your science teacher, the lab or the classroom you studied in? Even if it needs a little recollection, it's there buried somewhere in a dormant grey cell. A little more technically, the law of conservation of energy states that the total amount of energy in an isolated system remains constant. Consider space, through modern astronomy, the Hubble telescope, and the many giant telescopes around the globe, we have now have access to fascinating pictures and knowledge of the universe. There are massive galaxies hundreds of times bigger than our own, clouds of gas and dust, giant stars, each like a massive nuclear reactor, all brightly lit, active and alive. There is a massive universe out there, alive, active, even violent and loaded with energy. What if we could harness that energy? We can, but not from all those giant star systems, but from a simple star, our own Sun, a gigantic power house in itself, always at our disposal. Consider another force of nature, wind, the power of which inside a hurricane can destroy entire cities — wind that sweeps our landscape through the winter and helps us coin that lovely word called *wind chill*. How about nuclear, terrifying and fascinating, both at the same time?

And, finally, there is man, a little entity, the most intelligent, and yet almost powerless in the face of the power and fury of nature. Yet, like a little devil with a devious mind and through the power of it, man can wreck more havoc than any force of nature. So, what has mankind done to our planet, to Mother Earth? The fact that in the 21st century we are consciously talking green, global warming, and desperately trying to catch up with something called the *Kyoto Accord*, says that we have messed up big time and have woken up too late. With our knowledge of the universe, one would think by now we would have harnessed the massive power of the Sun's and the Earth's natural energies; declared oil as too messy and obsolete; and lived rich, comfortable, and luxurious lives from all that natural power at our disposal.

And, then, there are our little ones whom we the previous guilty generations are trying to teach to be green. Imagine my surprise one day in the daily morning rush when, not finding Nathan's regular metal water bottle, I strove to pack a plastic bottled water one. The lecture to me, an ever lecturing dad myself, from my grade 5 son, made me end the conversation with a meek and sheepish, "I'm sorry". I could not be happier for the school I chose for my son. The slogan at the Toronto Catholic District Board, in 2006, as we launched our green program was perhaps the one that struck deep within. It was both an admonition and a reminder of what our roles and responsibilities were, "We don't inherit the Earth from our ancestors, we borrow it from our children".

Through those mid years of the first decade of the 21st century, we were already living at a heightened conscious level of how fragile our earth had become. We were actively seeing its aftermath. Modern day green prophets like Al Gore were already winning the Nobel Prize for their work on it. The melting glaciers, the cracking and dispersing ice-shelves, the warming and rising oceans, shorter or longer winters, their severity or the lack of it, and so many other abnormal natural phenomenons should have normally scared the life out of us, just like the doomsday prediction. It didn't, it did scare the kids, though, as I gathered from the conversation between my grade 1 and grade 5 sons. When driving home one day, my younger son exclaimed, "I hope it becomes 100 degrees?" as we heard the weather report. The fascination with the number was short lived as I explained how no life would survive at that temperature on Earth. Needless to say my grade 5, earth-conscious-green son jumped in promptly with his doomsday prediction and lecture on how we were headed there if we did not change. Shutting him up, at the end of a long workday, using my exclusive Dad-bully powers was easy, then. But how true might that prediction be?

Move that clock to 2008, a little further down the decade to a man called Stéphane Dion. An academic with a great intellect, a man of unquestioned integrity, and also a man almost nearly always described with the words, ill-fated. So what was ill-fated about the ill-fated Dion? The fact that he lost an election on an issue he placed all his cards on? An issue that every single Canadian should have embraced wholeheartedly? The press described it as an ill-fated carbon tax plan or, as his adversaries described it, a tax-grab. Whatever the pros and cons of that green shift, the voters saw another tax, another burden. There are a host of arguments for and against it, but there was no disputing the fact that here was another add-on to an already overburdened voter paying a ton of taxes already. Take another leader, one of the first to introduce emission limits in a country where the automobile is the life of the nation and one of the leaders that made probably the largest investment in research for clean energy in the shortest time possible. We're of course talking of President Obama and the US. What did he admit during one of his election campaign meetings? Would the energy tax or the cap-and-trade introduce an additional burden on the taxpayer? Yes, it would. Would the price of electricity skyrocket? Probably, yes.

There is another weird notion, almost like a de facto misconception of life in North America. To be Republican in the US or Conservative in Canada is to be non-green, destructive, and an enemy of this planet. To be a Democrat or a Liberal means to carry the title of the good guys or simply the ones who care about the earth. And, then, there is the Green Party, the torch bearers of the green cause, still trying to win their first seat in Canada's Parliament. The concept is exactly as contained in the word, weird. Again, debatable, but that's where the issue lies. It is political football or soccer, where someone may brand the other as environmentally destructive and try and win an election by touting themselves as the green ones. Each of these parties and ideologies have their own adopted method, cap-and-trade, carbon credits, and so many others. There is always a dollar value to it. If you follow the many arguments for and against these, you will always end up with one final result. One way or another, the common man, the consumer, the voter will always pay for it.

Have you even questioned that concept, or did that one simple question always come to your mind? Why should you have to pay for it? Why is there always a dreaded dollar value to it? You pay your income tax each year, 15, 20, or even 25% each year, and then wait for the government to give you back something in your return. Like a meek lamb, without a single bleat, you agree to start paying a tax for your free –health coverage. And, then, vote Dalton McGuinty back to power in Ontario for him back to start a full 13% HST on everything. Did it matter that you would pay an additional 8% on your petrol and coffee? Each year, faithfully, you agree to keep paying the ever increasing property tax to the mayor, and so on in every part of the country, including the places where the carbon tax is already in place. You dumped your plastic grocery bags and moved to the cloth ones, probably a long time back. You started walking to the store for those little round the block trips. You started recycling every little bit. You changed your light bulbs to CFL. You insulated your house, lowered your thermostats in winter, raised them in summer, regularly inflated your tires and stopped idling your car. Ask the people around you, the common men and women that pay the taxes from their hard earned wages. They all have, not just in a few but in many ways. So, when the politicians say it's time to pay yet another tax, or pay an extra cent or two for green power, fuel, and everything else, what is your reaction? Did we just push back our green recovery by a few more years?

So, what is at the heart of global warming? We have all heard of Venus? An easy yes and In many contexts, Venus, the Roman goddess of love; those little pink razors and a host of products for women; the song by the group *Bananarama;* but, let's get right to the real one, the planet Venus. Sometimes referred to as our sister planet, today it is referred to as the classic example of what greenhouse gases could do. Once upon a time, this planet was supposed to have had an atmosphere and oceans like Earth, but a runaway greenhouse house effect took care of that. Today, it has an atmosphere laden with carbon dioxide and sulfur dioxide that create the strongest greenhouse effect, where no life can survive. What's the relation to earth? It is a phrase called *carbon dioxide emissions*, or, *carbon emissions* as it referred to in our green dictionary. Are we heading there? Maybe not for a few hundred million years, but that is at the heart of global warming. That is what all the drive is about — carbon emissions. The carbon dioxide that we produce from the daily use of our cars, air conditioners, and the power generated for us and our industries. The CO_2, along with methane and a bunch of greenhouse gases in our atmosphere, acts like a blanket trapping in the heat that should escape through the atmosphere. However, this is not a lesson on global warming, our kids would do a better job articulating it.

And so stands the simple question: Can we get rid of those carbon emissions? Not really. But, can we cut them down, or, can we bring them down to manageable limits? The answer to those and many similar questions is yes.

Yes. We have set achievable targets that let us breathe easier. We have scientific backing for these. We are investing in technologies that will help us curb our emissions. So, where might the problem be? Blame it on Scylla, or the lack of it, and the scientific community that has not made it possible. They have not discovered that technology – a technology where by using nuclear, solar, water, geothermal, and other renewable energy sources, we could generate unlimited power, or rather simply convert that limitless energy for our use. We could have unlimited power so that we don't have to run oil, coal, and natural gas based power generation plants. Net effect? We would eliminate about 40% of the carbon emissions, a huge step forward. Next step, use that power to create fuel cells, electric cars, re-electrify stations, and super energy technology that would wipe out all petrol and diesel engines. Oil would then be a dirt commodity, best left in the earth to exist as it did for hundreds of millions of years before we discovered it. Net effect, again? Another 30% of carbon emissions taken care of. That would leave our industries and other pollutants that we create. But then, with those kinds of advances, these would be mere footnotes to take care of, something like dotting the *i*s and crossing the *t*s.

These lines sound like a childish and dreamy oversimplification of an issue that is so huge and complex today. However, green independence still remains the subject that is the maker or breaker of elections, a central subject of debates leading up to those elections, a key component of election manifestos and, above all, a key topic political parties use to slam each other.

So, why the obsession with the political aspect for it when this should be a geological, scientific, and a natural resource issue? The answer lies, as always, in the hands that hold the reins of power. It is the government that can legislate and aggressively move the nation in a green direction. It is the government that can drive research in production of cheap green energy. It is the government that can legislate across the country on the largest polluters. Does there always have to be a dollar value attached? The murky answer to that: yes and no, and that is where we need to look beyond the immediate solutions. We have the scientific, industrial, and technical knowhow to manage our carbon emissions, so that in the next 30-40 years we can make a serious change for the better.

And so, going back to our sun, the wind, water, nuclear and so many other natural sources of energy that have no carbon emissions, that's where the answer lies. No solution is straightforward and simple. Through the massive stretches of empty land that North America has. From the dry arid sun-baked deserts in the south, to the cold arctic north hammered by the wind, there is a huge amount of energy to be harnessed. Where might the problem be? How would we get that power to our cities? Those power lines would have to run through nature reserves, forests, animal habitats and many others that have not been disturbed by man. While right next to us, near our cities are our power plants. The ones that generate over 40% of carbon emissions, the ones that run on coal, oil, and gas, the ones that burn all those fossil fuels and quietly supply almost 80% of our electricity. Villains we'd like to call them, or our work horses, yet they work tirelessly supplying power to our homes, offices, and cities. Will they go away? Not for a long time, as we discover abundant resources of coal, oil, and gas each day.

We might never have the Scylla technology, a Hollywood concept best left in the minds of those Hollywood writers. However, it is a peek into what is possible. A concept so similar to what people, many years ago, would have thought of flying, driving, and landing a man on the moon. We could have a green drive, aggressively led by the scientific community, and backed by the government, that would help research and create technologies that the common man could easily embrace. There will be sacrifices to make, or maybe not. We could aim for that ideal.

A simple example: the government in Canada was offering a five thousand dollar tax rebate for hybrid cars. Why so? Because the hybrid cars then cost an additional ten thousand dollars as compared to the regular ones. Why the stress on cars? Because automobiles and vehicles running on oil products contribute as much as 30% of the total carbon emission. A hybrid car would produce 80% less carbon emissions. So, what could the government do? Make hybrid cars mandatory? Yes, over a period. Could the government force every single manufacturer to make their cars hybrid? It could. We are already into the hybrid mode. What would happen to those extra thousands of dollars that the buyer would have to pay? With the focus on hybrid only, the cost of the technology would fall faster than ninepins. Take the example of a plasma television set. When it was first launched, it cost a whopping 25-30,000US dollars. What does it cost now, less than a decade later? A mere two to three thousand dollars! Laptop computers once cost thousands of dollars. We are now making the one hundred dollar laptops. Again, with the manufacturer being forced to sell hybrid only, they would be forced to invest heavily in that technology to make hybrids affordable for consumers or risk losing their business. What about the buyer? The buyer would actually pay for whatever carbon emissions were still generated. Importantly, it would actually eliminate the huge quantities of carbon emissions being generated. Compare that to a carbon tax on fuel without enforcing the hybrid or any green technology. It would mean an automobile driver would continue to pollute and generate those carbon emissions, but just would have to pay for it. Carbon tax without a green policy would simply be another license to pollute. Alternately, take the politicians, for example, the very ones that would institute a carbon tax. The ones who would jet set around the country during a campaign, create the carbon emissions, and then buy carbon credits for those emissions that could have been kept out of nature in the first place. Does paying the carbon tax and then polluting tell the Earth that these are licensed polluters, "Don't mind it"?! Aggressive research that leads to groundbreaking technology, enforcement of these viable technologies on industries, generation of abundant renewable energy, and protection of the consumer from bearing the final cost of this push, is the way we need to change our thinking.

There is a sensible way to our dream of a green earth.

It is a way that invites the citizens of the earth to join in spontaneously. And that would be a greater personal motivation than all the taxes and levies a government could pile on. In Canada, we already have the beginnings of the green revolution. How fast we accelerate to the finish can be a race against the rest of the planet. It can be a bar set so high that it forces the others to follow at a normal pace, and still get there, before it is too late. Renewal energy technologies that are already in place now like wind and nuclear power can be a great starting point. Today, nuclear power accounts for almost 20% of our power generation. In a country like France, with a population of 65 million, nuclear power supplies nearly 78% of their power needs. How long would it take us to ramp up our 20% to twice and then thrice that number? It can be a very quick ride, given our technical knowhow in that field, and with zero carbon emissions. Take the next largest culprit, our cars that we discussed earlier. Of the approximately 1.5 to 2 million vehicles sold in Canada annually, nearly half are cars and vans. Over the next 10 years, if we converted all those to hybrids, we would have taken another significant step and reduced our dependence on oil.

There is an even greater incentive if we are willing to change our perspective on the way to going green. Rather than tax, charge, and pay our way through it, we can enrich our citizens and country while getting there. The government can be a leader, with a helping hand rather than with a whip. That way is already known, and is espoused by those that are the green experts in our country. An investment of a few billions in public transit would generate tens of thousands of jobs. High speed, super efficient, point-to-point transit that ran on green power would make the use of automobiles an inconvenience. Examples like these already documented in the *Green Economic Stimulus Package* can generate thousands of jobs, while reducing carbon emissions and contributing to prosperity[xvi]. There are ways like these, all of which have a natural byproduct — a greener and cleaner earth. All these can happen while *greening* our country and the planet.

Perhaps, no greater inspiration to go green and to love and care for our planet can be found than from the ones that were the original inhabitants of this land — the Aboriginal people, the ones that have lived, sustained, and nurtured this land from time immemorial. As encompassed in these lines by the Chippewas of Nawash about themselves:

> *Along with indigenous peoples everywhere, our relationship with our traditional lands, waters and resources is profound, ongoing and an essential part of our identity and culture as well as the economy of our people that sustains us to this day. Who we are comes from the land. Our language comes from the land, our culture comes from the land, our sustenance comes from the land.*
>
> *Anything that nature provides must be respected, because then you are respecting yourself at the same time. There is a very strong obligation to respect the fact that we are all interconnected and interdependent*[xvii].

A New Canada

Politically Correct, or Incorrect?   155

Politically Correct, or Incorrect?

"We are a diverse nation", I remember

being told. It was one of the very first things I learned about Canada. "This is our unique difference, we retain our identity even while becoming Canadians, and unlike the great melting pot that New York or the US in general are". In the US, they said, you forget who you are and where you came from. I don't know how true that was but I never forgot that. In that first summer in Canada as I began my journey of discovery, I saw them all. White, black, yellow, brown, all those races that were so well represented. I saw the other colors, as well, that very multi-colored flag that represented so many others. It was a new beginning, a lot to learn, and it would take me a long time to realize and accept this diversity. As I discovered it, I began to feel a sense of pride in the truly diverse nature of this country. What's more, incident after incident proved to me that this indeed was a country that welcomed all.
As I went through those first critical months, starting life in a new country, it was such a big comforting factor. The "Hellos" were genuine, the answers to my repeated "Which way to…?" were long and detailed. It was the time when a new immigrant spends a lot of time on the job web sites, newspaper classified pages, as well as those long rental pages. It was, as they say, "starting life from scratch"'. I had to get a job, and I needed a place to stay, as my wife and son were to arrive soon.

Everyone had a word of advice, a ready hand to help, and a smile. That's one thing so rare and so good about us. The smile — you could get the warmest smile from a stranger on the coldest day and have the best summer day in the middle of winter. For me, for some reason, that took a lot of getting used to. "Why did that person smile at me?" I asked myself so many times. It didn't need an answer. This was Canada. Those warm summer days, those warm summer smiles built up what proved to be the best start anyone could have.

Perhaps, the one little incident that proved it beyond doubt was one of my first experiences of buying a newspaper. After having picked up jobs and rental magazines free, I discovered the newspaper stands outside coffee shops, subways, and the bus stops. I had no idea how much the newspapers cost or how that little box that dispensed newspapers operated. Seeing newspaper being sold from those self-help stands by the side of the road was enough to surprise me. I did manage to see the instructions up front, one day, as I ventured out to pick up one but then realized I needed change. As I ransacked my pockets, I heard the jingle of coins and from the open stand door out came two *Toronto Stars*. Soon enough, as I stopped my change-hunting charade and looked up, right there in front of me was a smile and a newspaper. "For you, Buddy", were the only words I heard. I don't remember even saying, "Thank you". It was too confusing. Maybe, there was no word said except that impression of the person walking away with his coffee. He was no rich dude, just an ordinary guy picking up his newspaper, and mine. It was worth a few quarters but the warm glow of that moment stayed with me forever. In my own little way, I tried to pass it on through the shopping buggies at the *No Frills* stores that I passed on, a few extra coins for the musicians at the TTC stations and, sometimes, for those bundles of humans lying wrapped by the sides of the streets. I am not sure if I succeeded in passing it on, but it kept that original glow in my heart warm and alive.

The shockers came much later, sad but true. I wished "*Merry Christmas*" and got a frown. "What's wrong?" I asked? "You have to wish *Happy Holidays*; you have to be politically correct". It was one of the saddest discoveries I made in Canada. Isn't December 25 all about Christmas, the day when Jesus Christ was born? So what if everyone does not believe? They don't have to; it could be just plain history. It is just plain acceptance and sharing of the other person, whatever their belief, whatever their creed. Would we be so violated if the man in front of us said, "*Eid Mubarak*" or "*Happy Hanukah*"? Would it outrageously destroy our sense of neutrality? Isn't it just plain joy and happiness oozing out of a person who might simply want to share it with everyone? A person simply celebrating his feast, his religion, or maybe all what his life and his faith is about? Above all, this is a person sharing goodness, peace, and love.

So, what does it mean to be politically correct? Is it defined in some holy text of political correctness? Who enforces it, and who decides the rules? The strangest question in all of this was screaming in my mind. Who do I need to be politically correct for? It is not defined. Yet, it sits like a monster, guarding some unknown holy grail or law to be enforced. Who are its keepers? Some unknown acolytes like the religious police in Saudi Arabia? Or, is it the new religion of secularism?

How much soccer do we play? A fair bit, yet not enough to be anywhere in serious contention on the world stage. Yet, it is the biggest sport the world over. When it comes to following the sport, we are right at the top. Take your mind back to any of the soccer World Cups in recent history. It is one of the biggest television audiences the world over. It stretches from the US down to South America, the land where soccer is poetry, to the tough lads from Europe, and then all the way through the Arab world, down to the lions of Africa, and the all the way east to Japan and, finally, down to Australia. Even our own diversity gets so well highlighted when hundreds of different national flags get adorned on cars during the soccer World Cup season. So, when that South Korean celebrates his upset victory over the Italians and honks his horn, does it outrage us? Is he politically incorrect? Did he violate our sense of hockey loyalty by looking at us and blaring his horn in soccer celebration, expecting us to do the same?

Perspective is such an amazing concept. It allows us to see the other in a context that would explain why the other would do what he or she did. We pride ourselves on so many facets of life that we have achieved victory over. We swear by *human rights*, civil rights, the rights of citizens, and even the rights of criminals and prisoners. Anyone who does not go by those standards is, in our dictionary, still in the Dark Ages. Take the example of the Iranians executing Derala Darabi in May 2009. Derala, not a hardcore criminal with a record, but a 17-year-old girl, was executed for an unproven murder, after a speedy sham of a trial. Whatever the background, our lives stood still for those few minutes as we contemplated the cruelty of that act. As always, as I followed the dialogue between readers of that online article, the word *barbarians* jumped out at me from one of the reader's responses. I totally empathized with it. That was, till I scrolled down that page a little further to a response to that response. It said, "Canada: 150,000 abortions; Iran: 0; ….who are the barbarians?"

And, that really got me thinking of the very diverse country I come from, India. Hindus, Muslims, Sikhs, Buddhists, Jains, Catholics, Christians, Jews, and so many other religions, all exist in peace and harmony. Sure, they have their share of communal riots and tensions. However, if one were to quantify that against the millions — totaling more than a billion — that live in peace, minute after minute, day after day, year after year, it would be a David v/s Goliath comparison. I grew up surrounded by all kinds of religions, learning about all the faiths, and happily accepting it as the most natural aspect of life.

Really, that one little fact made growing up in India so much fun. I attended a Catholic school with more 2000 students. However, truly symbolic of India, the Catholics in that school were a minority. The schools were managed by priests and nuns and there was no attempt to hide their Christian identity. When it was *Eid*, we promptly landed up at our Muslim friend's homes, wished them *Happy Eid*, and enjoyed their treats. When it was *Diwali*, or *Dussera*, or one of the many Hindu festivals, we were there promptly to wish them. It did not hurt a Muslim or a Catholic to wish the Hindu, "*A happy Diwali*" and be wished the same in return. Sure they all loved Christmas, all of them; it was the season of the rum cake. I am not sure how much rum our mums poured into those cakes, but they were all there, all my friends, ready to say the biggest *Happy Christmas*, and get to the cake. *Eid* brought its own share of hugs or the chest-hugs, as I like to call them. We all wished the Muslims and they all wished us. And during those long fasting days of *Ramadan*, we jumped right into the treats at the end of the day, or the big common plate full of *biryani* that they all shared. It was the most natural thing to do; we lived together; shared the same passion for sports, politics, and our country; and lived to prove that we were more brothers than friends. It was genuine, as genuine as the fact that each face on each human was uniquely different.

If your mind is being prompted to discuss this as ideal banter that existed at a buried simplistic level of society, then consider these two facts: India probably has the highest number of public holidays; naturally, based on the many religious festivals. Each of those holidays is a celebration of a different faith and its religious significance. What would you expect from a country that represents so many faiths? Right at the top of the political hierarchy is the President and then the Prime Minister. On each of those festivals, the President and the Prime Minister are out there with their wishes, "*Happy Diwali*", "*Eid Mubarak*", "*Happy Christmas*", and so many more. So, do that President and the Prime Minister violate the secular character of the country?

There is another beautiful custom; it has no name, it simply is that tray of sweets we sent and received on each festival. So, on each festival, you would see the festively dressed kids, busy going from house to house with plates of sweets covered with little white-laced cloths. And, the trays of meat, from the freshly slaughtered goats on *Bakri Eid*, it was so natural. There was a nice end to that practice, as the trays were emptied, with thanks, and returned; but they were never returned empty. Those empty trays came back with a few spoonfuls of sugar, at least. What it meant has no definition, but then it didn't need one. A little acknowledgement, a little thank you, a little peace, a little respect, a little acceptance, and a little sweetness. Whatever it may be, it cemented a society right at its core. If all that sounds a little distant, then simply take your mind back to the previous Christmas, and that coffee tin you left in your neighbour's mail box. Sure it said, "Happy Christmas", and maybe a lot more.

If you like, I have had the fortune of starting a new life in this country. Then, I'm sure you have your own little bag of stories that take you back nostalgically to those first days. I do hope your experience was as beautiful as mine, as I took my first steps in a new country, a new home. It was 1999, my first year in Canada and, incidentally, one of the years with very little snow. So, sadly for me, that first Christmas was not a white one. Disappointed as I was, I still remember how everyone in the IT department of the Toronto District School Board dragged me to the row of large windows as the first flurries of that year came down thick and fast, like beautiful giant puff balls. As I stared in awe at the sight of that fairy land stuff floating down from the skies, some very patient lessons in the differences helped me understand what flurries, flakes, black ice, and, then the awful bad ice storm, meant.

As they all stood around me, watching not the flurries but the awe in my face, I knew that big group of IT professionals were my first and lasting impressions of how wonderful it would be to live in Canada. Those little cautions about racial discrimination before coming here were quickly dispelled as gossip based folk tales. I remember Jay and Debbie planning an ambush when the first snowfall finally came. As Debbie led an unsuspecting me out of the door onto College street a barrage of snow balls smashed into my face and hair. When the fresh powdery snow did not hold up, hands full of it went inside my coat.

However, no memory is stronger and fonder than the Christmas surprise Jay and Debbie gave me on that first Christmas. No matter what your age, you always love a little surprise Christmas gift. Coming as it did from a group of colleagues, it made for some of the most nostalgic memories of settling in. A hockey stick, a puck, and a ball, could not have been more Canadian. What makes the memory sweeter is that Jay brought along his own hockey stick and, right there in that office, we pushed aside the computer-laden tables and played my first hockey game. I never discovered whether Jay and Debbie celebrated Christmas, religiously or otherwise, or if that larger group that consisted of a Chinese, a Pakistani, and some others from very diverse backgrounds, did. I do remember that we all went out and had a great Christmas lunch, wished each other *Merry Christmas* and *Happy Holidays*, and broke off for the holidays. It seemed like such a natural extension of the Christmas back in India.

Today, as we stand as a nation of 30 million, a quick scan of any urban community tells a startling story. We have lots of ethnic minorities and they are growing. They are growing to be very visible minorities. Those minorities are also mostly religious and are equally diverse in their religions. They are Catholics, Christians, Hindus, Buddhists, Muslims, and so many more from all over the world, all here in Canada. They are the future of this country; they are not going away. They will stay here, imbibe this Canadian spirit, and carry on the Canadian tradition. Have you wondered how that spirit gets passed on? If you were to look at some of the demographics of any classroom in Toronto, for example, it would take a huge leap of faith to tell a skeptic that this is the future, a classroom full of colors that represent scores of countries around the world. Get a white kid and a brown kid and a black kid and an Asian kid together from one of those classes, and you will see the kind of unity in diversity that exists. These kids don't see the color or the race, you can tell it in their friendship, their endless hugs, their chatter, their mischief, or even in their accent. That accent is probably such an insignificant factor to mention, but put it in perspective with the previous generation, their own parents, and the differences are so obvious. You would probably see a real life enactment of the famous Russell Peters Indian accent copy, and the pure Canadian accented kid. It speaks volumes about each new generation of Canadians growing together and learning to value the diversity that each different one brings to the classroom.

So, where is that Canadian spirit enshrined? Is it in a book, in an act, or in a charter? Sure, those exist, but not one that says that to be Canadian is to be first and foremost a nice person, a kind person, a warm person, maybe even a happy person? It is to accept the person next to you as he or she is irrespective of race, religion, or sex. That's basic humanity, you might say, just natural to be so. I don't think so. There is something more distinctly Canadian to it.

As saddening as the discovery of not being able to freely wish everyone a *Merry Christmas*, was the discovery on my first trip down south, to the USA. To that great democracy, the beacon of freedom, and so much more that it is proclaimed to be. They may be great in all that but, within a few minutes of crossing the border, the differences in human interaction were so starkly different you would think you had crossed over to another star system in some *Star Wars* episode. Blunt, arrogant, rude, were some of my first horrified reactions as we started to stop at all those highway gas stations. There were no smiles, no words exchanged, no conversations about the weather, or a simple friendly conversation with the attendants that manned the gas stations, fast food chains, and the toll booths. The simple *thank you* after having paid my gas bill received the most irritated look, even a suspicious one. I am sure it carried a hidden, softly muttered "Get lost"'. And I'm pretty sure, someone, somewhere, on that first US trip must have even said, "Damn Canadians". Generalization is a bad thing; but then, simply put, that is the way they do business in the US, so different from us.

As I returned from that first US trip, there was so much more to love my country for. There was enough time to throw in a lot more *hellos* and than*k yous*, there was always that extra minute to share a smile about the crazy fluctuating weather, and wait for the little extra smile your naughty toddler received from the cashier. It felt so good to be Canadian. So, in that simple principle of being Canadian, we can add that old adage, "Live and let live".

Somewhere, in the coming years, we need to redefine ourselves. We need to redefine ourselves as a land of many cultures, many religions, many faiths, yet one strong Canadian identity. Somehow, we need to get our heads around the fact that we are not a country of atheists or agnostics, and that deep down the majority of us that walk these streets carry a deep sense of faith in our very diverse religions. So, would we open our hearts, open our minds, let the greatness of our hearts, our magnanimity, and our sense of equality, and allow the bloke in front of us to say, "*Happy Christmas?*"

The Great Political Divide   167

The Great Political Divide

What defines us as Canadians?

"The true North strong and free," we sing with great pride. For all our sense of fairness, equality, and kindness, we are a proud nation. The list of all that we stand for, as proud Canadians, would be a very long one. Rightly so and, by no small measure, we would be an ideal for what can be achieved by a nation. In a long list of countries that the world is made up of today, we are at the very top. Politically, socially, and financially, we are proud of our achievements.

One of the greatest factors that define our greatness is our diversity. In my many years as part of the IT department of the Toronto Catholic District School Board, I loved to show off about one statistic that defined this diversity so well. In a department of a little more than a hundred people, we had as many as 39 different originating nationalities that spanned the globe in such a wonderful way. America, India, Italy, Portugal, China, Jamaica, Iraq, Iran, Indonesia, the Philippines, Peru, Brazil, Bangladesh, Ukraine, Belarus, Sri Lanka, Pakistan, etc.; you name it, we had someone. What struck me even more about the diversity in that department was that despite being the IT department of a Catholic Board, we had Hindus, Muslims, Jews, Christians, and probably a few agnostics and atheists, as well. Now thinking back, I wonder how common that may be, if one was to look across the many offices that fill our cities. We relish our diversity and, each day as that diversity grows, we welcome even more to join this large family. Naturally enough, this fact is reflected so well in our political world.

My first political realizations, on coming to Canada in 1999, inevitably go with the thought that those were the Chrétien years in Canada. Paul Martin was working his wonders with the deficits and surpluses, and Chrétien walked confidently into his third term on a challenge from Stockwell Day and a little push from Aline. I was politically ignorant in those first years. Coming from India, a Catholic, and part of a very small, yet vitally important and critical minority, voting for the Congress Party of India, the centrist political party came as a natural choice. And, so it came about that I threw in my lot behind the Liberals, wholeheartedly. As a landed immigrant, unable to vote, I cheered from the sidelines, celebrated their achievements, and felt the joy of the prosperity the country enjoyed. The road to discovering the right, the left, and the centre, was an interesting one.

Our political diversity, if one may define it as such, is what frames our political parties, the Conservatives, the Liberals, and the New Democrats. We call them ideologies, a critical part of our political process, blending and creating the balance needed. I'm sure you've been asked this question, sometime, as you've had a conversation with someone, your spouse in tow. "Do you guys fight?" a scary question for some newly weds. My answer has always been, "A lot; sure we do". I am no marriage counsellor, and Lynn and I have never had to see one, but somewhere in our 10 plus years of marriage I developed the following argument, when our tiffs got her down. "We're not two donkeys", I told her, "it's not as if one says something and both have to nod in agreement". And so, as loving spouses, we always reasoned it out and carried on even more united, and dedicated to our marriage.

Similarly, nationally, however deep our political differences go, we all stand united and determined in our dream to see Canada as the best. Out of our own visions, from our corners across the room, we dream one dream, of a strong and prosperous Canada. Despite our very radical stands, firmly set apart, deep enough for us to shout each other down, we understand that these are our political differences. We stand as one, all Canadians. Is this political ideology so deeply ingrained that it leads us to hate each other?

And so, discovering my political identity was one of the biggest and most challenging aspects of becoming a Canadian. As a Catholic, I so naturally believed that life begins at conception, that abortion is wrong — murder — that marriage is the union between a man and a woman, and so on. As I saw the *Our Father* weaned out of the classrooms, the mention of God in anything associated with learning a taboo, and so many other such facts, I took my first steps towards my political life. My first Conservative meeting was a real eye opener, compared to the images in my mind, formed from the sight of hundreds of thousands at political rallies. In India, political conventions and rallies came by the thousands, and supporters trooped in by the truck-loads, literally. Across the border, I saw the deeply ingrained political nature of the Americans, both the Republicans and the Democrats, and here I was at my first political meeting. In a large church hall, I could have counted barely 25-30-odd people and, within a minute of being there, I was offered the chance to be one of the delegates at the upcoming national convention. The reason? Simply because there weren't enough members present to be placed on the list. I came home that day a very sobered and thoughtful person. As the 2008 federal election came around, I campaigned actively with my local Conservative candidate. It was probably baptism by fire as I found the words, "Let's campaign at the subway stops" slipping out of my mouth. Despite the thumping heart, I realized I really wanted to do it and to gauge the political nature of this country. It was a truly memorable and learning experience. My riding, St. Paul's, in Toronto, was listed as one of the most educated ridings in the country because of the number of graduates and postgraduates that lived there. Standing outside the subway stations and bravely intoning, "Please vote Conservative", while handing out those bright blue flyers, was an education in itself. Pretty soon, I was already classifying people by their reactions. The loyal Conservatives gave me a *thumbs up*, the Liberals, a very curt, "No, thank you, it's Dion all the way", and the New Democrats, a big "Never, out with you capitalists", screamed right in my face. And so, in that election, I campaigned, became a *scrutineer* at a polling booth, saw the counting process, and discovered the magic of how democracy worked so smoothly in this country.

Yet, as time went on and I got to know more and more of my Conservative friends, I realized I was so different ideologically. As I got to know more and more of the local Conservative group, I realized that not everyone was socially conservative, the primary reason I joined. So many of the rest were fiscal conservatives. Me? I was not so sure. "So you're not socially conservative", I asked a pretty young member of the riding at one of the pub nights. "No, and I am definitely pro choice", was her firm affirmation, and I felt something give way in my Conservative fervour. Another afternoon, in early March 2009, as we elected a new local board, I heard one of the national councillors speak and he said, "Let's be clear, governments do not create jobs". It was the 2008 recession and the new stimulus package was all about government money creating jobs and stimulating the economy. I loved the action plan, even though many Conservatives probably held their noses as they backed the plan. It took me back to another great leader, Ronald Reagan, and the words,

"Government is not the solution to our problem; government is the problem". Yet, my mind screamed at the absolute absurdity of it. Why then do we elect governments and entrust them with billions of our dollars? Why do they hold the key to the treasury, if they don't carry the responsibility to see that all is well for each and every Canadian in this country?

In my own little dreams for Canada, I realized that there was no perfect fit. If I was looking for a political nest that was a perfect ideological, social, and fiscal home, I did not fit, either with the left, or the right, or the centre. Whether socially or fiscally conservative, that was my conservative diversity.

The same Canada over the years, slowly, also taught me that this country, with its beautiful *Charter of Rights and Freedoms*, belonged to the religious and the atheists, to those of the evolution theme and to those of the creation theme, to the gays, the lesbians, and the heterosexuals, and to those on the right and the left. It was a slow and late, mellow warmth that one day told me that I had learned that I could still continue to be a Catholic, an openly staunch Catholic with my beliefs intact, and still be accepted, without having to hide my beliefs. It also taught me that the others did not have to fear me, or look for a secret hidden agenda in my plans. It suddenly gave me the strength to openly profess my beliefs and not worry about being pounced on by everyone who considered themselves forward thinkers. I had to grudgingly accept that my thoughts were termed in the main stream as *backwards*. Why not higher, I asked myself? North America was still over 60% conservative in thought, and religious by nature, I read around the same time.

In those years, I also realized that I could be a politician with a deeply religious Christian view, with a passion for science, and the scientific community did not have to fear that or feel threatened by it. It gave me strength to know that Canada accepted me for what I was, and I in turn accepted everyone for what they were, regardless of religious, political, sexual, or any other diverse belief. It also told me that I could be in the government and do a lot of good things, besides holding up my hand and saying abortion was wrong and see five others raise their hands and say, "It was the right of the mother to choose". And, as in a democracy, we could all have a talk over it and carry on with life. Above all, contrary to belief, society did not have to fear someone whose life was grounded in the religious principles of "Love thy neighbour as thyself".

And so, it still left me with the thought: Did I have to belong to a fixed political view or agenda? Did I have to be fiscally conservative and follow those principles rigidly or be a New Democrat and believe in those principles? Were balanced budgets and small governments the answer, or was taxing and spending the answer? The answer was clear: It did not matter. As a politician, all I cared for and worried about was whether I had a heart for Canadians. Did it matter to me if people had jobs; if the children had food and education; whether people were poor and hungry; if everyone had good health care; if crime was on the wane in our cities; whether we prospered; whether we generated enough wealth to reinvest in our people and if that in turn generated greater wealth? That was what my government was about. That was all that mattered to others.

From the many months and years I spent in the Middle East, there was one feeling I came away with, as did most expatriates, you feared the *Shurta*, or the local police. They were not mean or tyrants, just plain cops; but for some unknown reason the moment an expatriate saw them, they went into hyper caution mode. That probably set us apart so distinctly from the locals Arabs. If the locals could not outdo the expats in a lot of things, this was one in which they took great pride. Perhaps, the greatest manifestation of this came during the driving tests. Getting a driving license in the Middle East was equivalent to earning a degree. It was basic to job security, to mobility, and probably carried as much weight as a college degree from back home. Nowhere was the fear of the *Shurta* more magnified than during those driving tests. "What is so scary about that khaki uniform", my driving instructor, a local Arab, of course, screamed at me for the umpteenth time, as he prepared me for my second attempt. "You expats freeze when you see the *Shurta*", he said throwing up his hands in despair. He was hardly exaggerating. Well, you had to fear them if you wanted to pass, because they simply tricked you. As you drove along the city roads, as part of your driving test, following their instructions and your own driving lessons, carefully, they would take you right up to a *No Entry* lane and say, "Turn in". Worse still, you would be at red signal and they would scream, "Come on, keep moving". It did not take long to fail those tests. Do you remember your own Canadian driving test? I remember it so well. I probably would have hugged the examiner as he told me, "There are no tricks here", as we started out on our test. The rest of the test was like a drive with a friend, alert and watchful, as I told him my *Shurta* story. In the true Canadian way, we finished that test, as a matter of business, and I jumped back on to the TTC, dreaming of my first car in Canada.

I remembered that line for a long time and can picture it to this day. "There are no tricks here". There are no tricks in real Canadian life except, of course, if you stepped into the world of politics. As I became politically involved, I discovered the most interesting section of any political article that I read on the web was not the article itself but the reactions, the online responses, and the dialogue that followed. Some of it was pure hatred, seething hatred, from one set of followers to the other. It's probably a North American thing, as you see it even more if you were to follow the same course for the American followers of the Democrats and the Republicans. One day, as I stood in a line at a local *McDonalds*, a noisy grumpy customer slowly started to get under my skin. His constant tirade about the state of affairs of the country portrayed a sad and poor Canada. It was the time when Stéphane Dion, Jack Layton, and Gilles Duceppe were putting together their coalition, in 2008. I finally turned back to him and asked him what his solution was. "Shoot Harper", he yelled, as the whole place fell into an eerie silence. Delighted with the audience he had gained, he yelled even louder, "Shoot Harper; we will be all fine". He was by now ready to explode and, luckily for me, someone from across the room yelled, "And the *Raptors*". There was an instant rapport there, and the two of them, I am sure, downed many burgers and Coke that day. But it left me thinking of that deep hatred we see, sometimes.

I am not going to extol the virtues of any political party or of any political leader in this country. Somewhere along the line, we have lost the sense of political rivalry and, however little we may admit it, there is a Canada that pits the East against the West, or the many newly defined divisions, in so many ways. We have such a huge political divide. We don't just believe in it; we live by it. We have such great classical terms to label each other; the right, the left, the centre, the left of centre, and the right of centre. We inherently believe that each carries its own agenda. We have forgotten that it is an ideological divide that we need, that we should cherish. Is that not what democracy is all about, a diversity of thought, a diversity of opinions, a plethora of thoughts and agenda that seek to attain the same goal by different means? How can we then not find a central ground?

Have you visited the website of any political party? It is probably ironic that the greatest exposure to the opposing leader is not on his own website but on the rival one.

Stéphane Dion, during his short ill fated tenure as he led the Liberals through some very disastrous days, graced the welcome page of the Conservative website more than Stephen Harper. Even the great McCain-Obama race, despite all the pledges of a clean campaign, threw enough dirt around. So, is it the political parties that are such, or is it that we people need that kind of negativity to make up our minds? Over and over again, all the political pundits have declared, at the end of the day, that those negative ads work, one way or another. The Conservatives call it Liberal hypocrisy, and the Liberals call it the Conservative war machine. Whatever the label, it's a sad way of doing things.

Have you seen a typical question period in the House of Commons? It is the one of the most vibrant symbols of democracy, as the ruling and the opposition benches fulfill their role. However, tune into any political discussion on your television station and the descriptions of that hour by the very best of political pundits will make the most ardent supporter of democracy cringe. Sometimes, it is an absolute disaster in terms of intelligent debate, and the attacks that each set of parliamentarians level at each other would be like street fights. Some of the descriptions I picked up one night from the CBC panel describing question period, and those partaking in it, were words and descriptions like "incompetent", "impotent", "it's an institutional problem", "attempt to shine in front of the camera", and "outrageous". "Why do they have to shout and always be in an infuriated state?" was a question that got the wittiest answers. Perhaps the one statement that put a sorry stamp on that whole affair came in the words, "Nothing that happens there changes the price of bread!"

We bash each other to a point of hatred. Just read some of the follow up comments at the bottom of those political articles. The left is evil, they will tax and spend; the right has a hidden agenda, a deep secret one; and the centre, everyone wants to be there, because isn't that where the votes are. India, one of the world's largest democracies, is represented by over 500 Members of Parliament. There are bitter rivalries, there is political violence, and there are the odd cases of violence in parliament itself. The competition to get to those 500 seats in parliament from the billion that live there is fierce. Yet, as one TV commentator once exclaimed, if only the people could see the fun and friendship these 500-odd men and women enjoy during recesses.

Doing business by the power of fear rather than by the spirit of cooperation is probably the way we go. Stephen Harper, despite a pretty much rule from the centre, was accused of transacting business with the threat of no confidence votes and the threat of an election over the heads of the opposition. Again, despite a minority government, but a clear swing in the Conservative direction, the opposition clearly set out to topple the government within three months of the election in 2008. What was Michael Ignatieff's first declaration after taking over the leadership of the Liberals? "Reform the EI or face an election!" All this at a time when the world was at the peak, or rather the lowest ebb, of the recession and all the common Canadian simply asked was, "Fix the economy". So, did our leaders ever think that they could form a joint committee of economic experts and take their lead on how to handle the sagging economy? It probably would have worked and there would have been so much credit to go around that any of those leaders could have dreamed of a majority, when the elections finally came around.

So, did the Liberals bring down the government during that summer of 2009? Overwhelming public opinion during that period said NO to an election. No one wanted a ruined summer; no one wanted another few hundreds of millions wasted in less than a year; no one wanted government to come to a stand still; and most of all no one wanted politicians playing stupid ego games when there was just one issue on the table, the economy. It was probably the most human fact, a very elementary one at that, which should have decided the matter. One that simply would have said that as the stimulus money began to reach the ground, it was providing the much needed jobs and, if not everyone, at least thousands of construction workers that summer would have a pay cheque and food to put on the table. Yet, despite that fact, the left merrily sabre rattled and, without a shred of doubt, declared their intention to vote against the government. In all of that, two men did something that probably would be a political science lesson for a long time. Stephen Harper, the Prime Minister, and Michael Ignatieff, the official opposition leader, sat across a table, once, twice, thrice, and talked, set out an action plan, and formed a blue-ribbon panel to study the EI issue. The panel, truly representative of both parties, besides their own MPs, had an expert from each side. That was true democracy at work, not a political divide but a political unite.

That Government in Ottawa 181

That Government in Ottawa

Ever so often, I receive a letter from my Member of Parliament. It lists out her work, current assignments, achievements, and a whole lot of stuff that I grudgingly would love to term as "Job well done". It also lists out her public engagements along with some very nice photographs. As of this day, as I write these lines, I have lived in Canada and, for the most part, at my current address for about 10 years. Yet, in all these years, I have never met my Member of Parliament. I suppose it could be my fault for not attending all those public engagements, or for not following the political scene closely enough so as to get a chance to say hello. Do I need to be in touch with my MP?

What is your impression of your Member of Parliament? A nicely suited, dignified looking man or woman, chauffeur driven, who walks down the halls of parliament, earns a great salary, enjoys some nice perks maybe and, of course, returns every four years or earlier as a "lawn sign". We have over 300 members of parliament and over 30 million residents of this country. To expect this handful of people to be in touch with every one of us is near impossible.

So, who really is your MP? I am not sure how to define it, but I suppose this person is one of the many public figures that come into our lives once in a way, asking for our votes, mostly, and then goes back to the comforts of that exalted life.

That is a false exaggeration, and I know they work hard up there in Ottawa but, still, those wonderful people in Ottawa, they seem so far.

I once had the privilege to go to Queen's Park at the height of the SARS epidemic as part of the *Open Doors* events. I was simply awed by the grandeur and history within those walls. "This is the seat of Ernie Eves", my guide explained, as I looked in wonder. It took my mind to my own MPP. I've never met this person either. I'd love to meet them both, the MP and the MPP, and ask them to walk my streets sometime. Just to see them as a commoner, just to see them in touch with reality, or maybe just to know that the politician that represents me is not some exalted royalty, not a concept, but a real person with flesh and bones. If you were to look up the Legislative Assembly of Ontario on the Internet, here is what you would find about our elected members.

> *A Member's day will typically be divided among participating in the business of the House, attending caucus and committee meetings, speaking in various debates, or returning to his or her constituency to address the concerns, problems and grievances of constituents. Depending on personal inclination and political circumstances, some Members concentrate most of their attention on House matters while others focus on constituency problems, taking on something of an ombudsman's role in the process*[18].

One of the first people I ever spoke to about politics was a truly great person, and one with vast professional experience. With knowledge, wisdom, and experience oozing out of every single strand of his silver hair, he taught me about so many great things associated with education in Canada. He was an educator at heart, and held many esteemed positions, including Director of Education for some school boards in Ontario. After a long and distinguished career, he was approached to be the candidate for a leading political party. With his failing health in mind, and the demands of a busy career as a politician, he declined. They had told him that, as a politician, he had to be ready for a very hectic life. He was told he would always be wanted for events, inaugurations, speeches, etc. Well, that was one aspect, and that struck me as really strange, strange but true. I had always imagined an MP's life as very hectic, but hectic doing a lot of social service. A personal life challenged by the rigors of always being available to the people.

In India, where I come from, some of the best cartoons come around elections time. A typical one would depict a half bent, bones-sticking-out poor peasant, outside a small hut and a dried-up field, being greeted by a politician. In contrast with the extreme poverty of the peasant in the picture, an army of security personnel, gun toting commandos, photographers, and the inevitable line of cars surround the politician. Oh, and not to forget, a helicopter somewhere in the background for good measure. "You're back for my vote", says the poor peasant in the call out, "didn't you come here four years back and promise me a long list of things?" The picture of the peasant and the politician in the flashback frame from four years ago is exactly the same. The same poor bent-over peasant, the same parched field, the same hut, except, of course, the politician who looks a good forty pounds lighter. You know the rest. But that little cartoon was so true, election after election.

How about our politicians? At the end of Paul Martin's short tenure, the liberals went into the elections with the sponsorship scandal hanging round their necks and a not too promising scenario ahead. That was the rare time I saw some big time politicians, veterans of Ottawa, walking the streets, knocking on doors, at Union Station in downtown Toronto, and giving it their best shot. So, why do we send these 300-

odd people to parliament? Of course, to legislate, to debate and discuss the issues facing the country, and to keep our democracy alive! Isn't that what democracy is all about?

I still cannot see it as a complete picture. Remember Carol Huynh, the Olympian from Hazelton, B.C.? My reference is not to Carol's Olympic quest but to another line from that article:

> In Hazelton and its surrounding hamlets and reserves, the chance to support an aspiring athlete brought together communities for whom economic deprivation is common, and tragedy only too familiar. The hardships have been ignored, even if only temporarily, as they have cheered on one of their own doing battle half a world away.

Remember, we also spoke of suicide among these youth. *Economic deprivation*, *Tragedy,* and *Suicide* form a sad but real picture of people, real people on the ground, driven to despair by an economic situation hardly under their control. So, again, my question, "Where was their MP, and what did he or she do for them?" And then, again, is it really the MP's responsibility? Maybe he or she did really care; maybe he or she really helped them. How far did that buck pass? How far along the line did an MP, a government, there in Ottawa, decide to look into not just Hazelton but hundreds of little Hazeltons that needed jobs, that needed pay cheques, so that people would be able to live, so that ordinary people would be able to put food on their dinner tables?

So, here is a picture of an MP of a downtown core, could be Toronto, from Sherbourne Street to Yonge Street along King Street and Queen Street. Somewhere down there where you would find the rich and the poor, the offices and the pubs, the prayer groups and night clubs, the revelers and the peddlers, the fancy food restaurants and the fast food ones, and one large humanity of people going about nocturnal tasks to fulfill their duties of the night. Did that MP get to meet those by the wayside, high on drugs and alcohol, streets lined with prostitutes, and halfway houses desperately trying to save a few? Would this MP walk down those streets in the dark of the night, see for himself the life of these forgotten ones first hand, and then again, in the day, walk the rows of houses in the back streets, and talk to people one home at a time, one street at a time, and then armed with that firsthand knowledge go back to Ottawa, and do something about it?

Is it the responsibility of Carol's MP to fight for investment on behalf of his or her people, to create jobs, to do his or her own bit to help people through their economic hardships? Did Carol's MP use that desperate scenario to push legislation, business reforms, and any possible tools to encourage businesses to invest in these forgotten places? Most of all, did Carol's MP have time to meet his or her constituents, a few at a time, a few each weekend, and then understand them, their problems, and let them feel the goodness of having spoken to someone who may have a real chance to do something about it? And, right across Canada, did these people, those 300-odd men and women who hold the real power over the purse strings and legislation, do something real about it?

Remember those beautiful old stories of mighty kings and generals that walked the streets in disguise at night, dressed as poor men, getting down to their subjects to know what life outside their palace was and to know firsthand the problems of their subjects? Would our leaders walk those routes? Would a prime minister or minister or a premier walk those crime and drug-ridden streets? Would any of them walk the streets of downtown Toronto and simply peek at the life of the common people? Would an MP or MPP walk with those who worked not one but two or three jobs a day and still found themselves struggling to make ends meet? Would you rather see that picture, or would you rather see a prime minister surrounded by an army of black-suited –secret service men, with little white-coiled wires sticking out of their jackets and into their ears, their eyes scanning as many as they could? In February 2009, as the Prime Minister and the Premier stood on one of the GO station platforms announcing a huge investment in infrastructure, did you see a few hundred construction workers ready to shake their hands and launch them on to their shoulders? Sadly, you would see a huge gap, a real physical gap between the lines of people, if there were any, and our leaders.

Across the world, our leaders are forced to live behind a wall of security, a wall that literally puts a huge physical gap between them and the very people they serve. How long does it take to get close enough to a head of state, or how many barriers do you have to cross? How many personal body checks, metal detectors, and agents do you cross before you see the person who you chose to serve you, the people?

My little stress on what the military calls, "boots on the ground", may sound farfetched. But, is it? One day, during a busy lunch hour, as I waited to meet my wife at the corner of Queen Street and Yonge Street, I saw a well dressed lady walk past me, very formal and dignified in her look. You could tell she was out for a little lunch break, a brisk walk, but not in any particular hurry. Her glances in all directions, at people, at life happening at a very brisk pace in that downtown stretch, somehow told me she seemed like that disguised queen taking a measure of real life. It also struck me that she looked strangely familiar. As I gathered my thoughts, and looked after her, it struck me that she bore an uncanny resemblance to the then provincial minister of education for Ontario, Kathleen Wynne. In a flash, I was running after her, and a few panting breaths later, caught up with her. "Excuse me, but are you Kathleen Wynne?" I asked her. "Who might that be?" she asked me, most unperturbed, still that serious look. By now, I knew I had goofed up, and if she didn't smile soon enough I would have to be ready with my multitude of apologies. "The education minister. Aren't you the one?" I said. "Don't you wish?" she exclaimed, and broke into the biggest of smiles. I didn't have to worry, as I said sorry and simply turned away, a little disappointed. I had wanted to thank the minister for the wonders she and the premier, Dalton McGuinty, were doing for education in Ontario. Kathleen Wynne, of course, was busy that day, very busy, redrafting an offer for the public elementary teachers union of Toronto, so that there would be no strike and no outages to the business of educating thousands of public school elementary kids.

So, the question remains, why my big obsession about being in touch with the common man? Well, take it metaphorically. From whom do the leaders take their cue? The Han dynasty in China existed around 221 B.C. It was one of the greatest ancient dynasties the world has known. Its founder, Han Gaozu, ruled on a simple principle, inspired by the philosopher XunZi:

> *The Prince is the boat;*
> *the common people the water.*
> *The water can support the boat, or*
> *the water can capsize the boat.*

In 2008, as the world headed into a recession, Stephen Harper came back, re-elected with a slightly larger mandate, not big enough to be an absolute majority. The message from the voters, a clear one — it was not a blank cheque. It was the first time I actively campaigned for my local Conservative candidate. Those were my first infant steps into the world of politics. The US was already losing jobs by the millions and, as that big ocean liner rocked from side to side by the waves of economic downturn and uncertainty, we watched from our safe shores. Ours was an armored frigate securely moored to the docks. Slowly, as the waves got bigger, we watched, concerned but still optimistic that we would ride out the storm. As the job losses mounted, as the factories closed, the budget that should have become an instant point of unity for all political parties to help out a hurting nation became a source of instant discord. It instantly united the opposition into a coalition to overthrow a government, less than three months after the elections. For a country heading into recession, the focus shifted to partisanship and the termination of funding to floundering opposition parties. As a registered Conservative, I sat back and thought of the hundreds that were losing their jobs, an economy already sputtering, and a nation headed towards a plain recession. Would not this be the time to really get down to the grassroots and offer a real helping hand to people? With the US government already having a $700 billion stimulus plan in the works, the path ahead would be so amply clear for two economies so closely linked. In plain human terms, I thought, what greater opportunity could there be for all politicians to fan out as one, across the nation, and build a bridge between parliament and the real financially hurting citizens? This was the perfect opening to open up a dialogue with a real good handshake, with a helping hand to those skeptics and opponents alike. In plain human terms, here was an opportunity to really help people. And so, my question, did our elected representatives still go after each other or put aside their differences and get in touch with the common man? Was that budget a Conservative budget that the opposition simply saw in regular terms as one to be criticized? Did the government see an opportunity and a need to have a total consensus budget? Why do our politicians wait and watch and then act and always play catch up? When Michael Ignatieff threatened the Conservatives with an election in

June 2009, did they have a plan? The 360 hours stipulation went off the table even before the discussions began. The left, they had a proposition, but all they targeted was voting out the government. Four parties, sitting together, would have rendered desperately needed help to thousands of unemployed that summer, rather than a panel studying those recommendations that summer.

How much do we spend on the security of the Prime Minister and other senior leaders? What would happen if they got on to a commercial flight, the first one available for Toronto, or Calgary, or Vancouver? And then, would they simply grab a taxi to the nearest venue of their event or would they have the entire stretch of the 401 or the 427 closed for the convoy? Would we see a day when the Prime Minister, or the local MP, or a minister, took a drive and sat by one homeless person at a time, on those downtown exhaust grills that warm these homeless people and, with an army of volunteers, social workers, etc., got those people off the street? Does it sound so farfetched or weird? Sitting with a homeless person on a warm grill may sound scary to most Canadians. So, how about paying a visit to a few of the hundreds laid-off car plant workers down in Oshawa? A simple question of how it felt to lose a job that the person held for 20 years or so, or how is the next mortgage payment going to be handled, or can we speed up that EI process? Does it sound like the thinking of an idealist or a lunatic? Or, does it sound like the thinking of a leader with a heart and a genuine desire to see every one cared for? Would we try to frame the question as a Conservative or a New Democrat, and find a rationale for or against a type of thinking we may label as socialist? Or, would we simply accept the reality of a family facing an uncertain tomorrow? What would a politician do as he drove along, or rather got driven along a busy street for an event at the Fairmount Royal York Hotel and saw a group of homeless people huddled under a makeshift plastic tent? Remember those tent cities that got thrown out? So, would this politician have the courage to have the convoy pulled over and walk over to those homeless and, right there under the frigid sheets of plastic, offer a hand to do something about it, or maybe just understand their point of view? I'm sure life would look very different from that perspective.

When did we lose touch with our own government in Ottawa? When did the government lose touch with us, the common folk? When would be the day, when the government aided by armies of financial experts, and social workers, and the hundreds of organizations and food banks that keep those on the fringes of society alive, get right down to business? One little dream, one little step down, one little hand shake, one little thought is all it takes.

Are you the proverbial "bread winner" of your family? Do you take that deep pleasure at the end of the day in seeing your little ones happily fed, bathed, and tucked into bed? Then, picture yourself in place of that worker who packs up one final time and heads home from a lockout. Picture yourself in place of those hundreds that walked home in those tough months of 2008 and 2009. Picture yourself in those forest industries that simply shut down. Picture yourself in those remote communities when losing one job would produce the sad depressing reality that, in that little town, this was the end. Picture yourself looking at that only factory in that little town, watching it close shop for good, that one centre of work and livelihood gone. And so, where do you go from there?

Remember the concept of the control room on *CNN*? Picture yourself in the control room of a nuclear arsenal where you monitored and responded to every single blip. Wouldn't you think that with all the resources at the disposal of the government, with the advancement in technology, and with the power of our financial brains, we would have control rooms where experts would not just watch events but be hyper pro-active in forecasting those events? Can you picture a control room called laid-off or unemployed, with a big red beacon blinking in every spot of the country where they laid off a mass of people, or where another business shutdown?

Is our government a large behemoth beast that lives there in Ottawa? Is it like that mythical capital of a large civilization up in the heavens that every time its subjects look up in the sky they fall on their knees? It's time we took back our government. It's time we established a hot line to our government and they did the same to us. There are many countries in this world that are shining beacons of democracy, the US, Canada, England, and India, to name a few. Are these democracies there to exist as ideals of what mankind has achieved?

We have to dream and believe in a day when every single MP gets back to his or her riding, at every single opportunity, has time to get to know every single one of his or her constituents, has time to sit if not play a game of basket ball with youth, who might otherwise be hanging out in malls or getting into fights or simply planning how to finance the next joint? We have to dream and believe in a day when weekends and other off days from Ottawa will be the busiest days for MPs, as they get back to their real bosses, the people, and stay abreast of every little problem that plagues their constituents?

A Higher Calling 195

A Higher Calling

In his comedy talk show *Red, White and Brown,* Russell Peters has a joke about how he hates soccer. The reason? Simple. Neither of the two countries he identifies with, India and Canada, are ever in the World Cup. Canada, for obvious reasons. It is a *world event.* We don't get involved in world events. The joke goes on. We look at the US. Are you guys going? Go ahead, that's great! We'll stay back; we'll tidy up. It's just a joke. And, basing an opinion on it is stretching it. Isn't humor based on life, especially the humor of stand up comedians?

We, Canadians, are nice; too nice; too sweet; so sweet that we have become content to take a back seat and let others lead. We're happy to let others take the glory, and follow contentedly. When was the last time we led on the world stage? When was the last time a Canadian leader stepped right out and took over the mantle for peace in the Middle East, or a dialogue with the "Axis of Evil Nations", or peace with Libya? We're happy to leave it to the superpowers! Really, what's the difference between them and us? Are we poor? No. Are we backward? No. Are we illiterate, no? Are we technologically inferior? No. Are we undeveloped? No. The answer to those, and many more, is a big NO. We are right up there. But we lack the political and social will, internally and externally.

Maybe, it's something to do with the big neighbor down south. The big mighty US, a true world superpower and, after the collapse of the Soviet Union, perhaps the only one. Probably, that's the reason why. Maybe, it's just that we are so used to living right next to the big mighty US, and hearing half the world news about them, that we dare not even lift our heads. We love to bash them, though. We love to criticize them; call them rude, arrogant, and a lot more things. It makes us feel good about ourselves, about our goodness, our sense of justice, and our sense of peace. Maybe, we don't want to be disturbed from our pedestal, some hypothetical pedestal we have installed ourselves on.

So, is it worth losing it? Is it worth taking a stand on worldly issues? Is it worth sticking our hands out? Take the example of the French President Nicholas Sarkozy during Israel's bombardment of Gaza in 2008. The French had as good or no connection to the conflict, or a connection like any of the rest of the world, to the strife in the Middle East. Yet, he was there, talking, negotiating, flying from country to country, and doing his bit for a ceasefire. What did Canada do? Sure, we took what we believed was a just stand. We released an official statement and made our stand clear. We did have a lot at stake. We had a whole lot of Canadian citizens stranded in Gaza. We had a lot of action, internally; supporters of the Palestinians came out in large numbers to protest the attack. Israel's supporters came out in just as large numbers and defended Israel's right to defend itself and guarantee its safety. Yet, did we believe that we could stretch out a white flag for both sides to notice and take on the mantle of peacemaker? Did we believe that there was so much to be achieved from the devastation that would add a chapter of peace and maybe trigger a peace process for the Middle East?

January 20, 2009, was probably one of the red-letter days in history, not just the history of the US, but of the world.

A HIGHER CALLING

The US installed its first African-American president. It was a world political event that captivated the entire world like no other. Millions of people around the world watched and celebrated as if their own president had been installed. Here, in Canada, there was nothing short of frenzy. Schools, offices, malls, pubs, and every possible public place, had television sets beaming the inauguration live. While many watched it at work, some Canadians actually took the day off to stay home and watch history being made. If that was not enough, some even drove down to the US to be a part of history.

Ironically, or sadly, our elections and the campaign preceding them, happened around the same time. While the US election galvanized every citizen, in what was billed the election of the century, we quietly went about our own. Sure, it was a great campaign. Yet, despite the election fever in the air, we had probably one of the lowest turnouts, yet again. Our election news ruled the airwaves, totally, for a few days at best. And then it was back to the rest of the world, and probably back to the impending US election. I remember driving home on the actual US Election Day and so many FM channels took time to stop their music and wait for that historic announcement. Some even had a countdown to the end of George Bush. What did it matter to us?

One factor that was so instrumental in the change that swept the US was the power of the youth. No leader in the past had inspired youth to come out and shoulder their responsibility, as this one. It was the age of social networking, and youth from coast to coast responded like never before. With their little contributions of five and ten dollars, their door to door campaigning, registration of new voters, tea parties, and their zeal, and by their sheer presence, they changed the course of their nation to something they wanted. If you were to visit the Elections Canada website at the same time, here is what you would read

> *A study commissioned by Elections Canada on the rate of participation at the 2000 general election showed that younger Canadians were voting at significantly lower rates than older electors. For the 2004 general election, Elections Canada conducted a study that cross-referenced actual votes with data from the National Register of Electors to find out how many people were voting in each age group. The results showed that approximately 37% of electors aged 18–24 voted. For the 2006 general election, a similar study showed that approximately 44% of electors in the 18–24 age group voted* [xix].

So, how do we get our youth out? How do we get them involved in social issues, in elections, in directing and controlling the future of this country, their own country? If you were to look closely at the youth around you, your kids, nephews, nieces, neighbor's kids, you would see that proverbial apathy. But only a fool would not notice the quiet fire that needs but one spark. Working at a school board gave me a unique opportunity to see youth in action in so many ways. One event, CSUNA or Catholic Schools United Nations Assembly, based on the UN theme, had youth from schools grouped into delegations representing the various countries of the world. To any observer watching them, it was a fascinating event symbolizing youth participation. As I walked past the atrium that day, I saw these youth wild and animated, deep in debate and action on every possible issue that we need them fired up on. The UN, world peace, *Going Green*, volunteering in Africa and other poor nations, these kids had it all. They even had their own litany of resolves ending with the now immortal, "Yes we can!". Yet, where did they vanish during the elections? Where are they when we need them right at the forefront, shaping their own destiny, as they shape the destiny of this nation? Somewhere along the line, we need to find them, inspire them, and bring them on

A HIGHER CALLING

board as the most important stakeholders of the future.

There is a niceness to us. Niceness in the way we do things, the way we project ourselves, the way we respond to international issues, the way we quietly do our assignments around the world. Remember Afghanistan, the forgotten war of the US? How it became our baby? We did it, and did it very well. As a true peace keeping force, we shed precious Canadian blood and helped an infant democracy take its first steps. It's nice and commendable. It wins us a lot of praise and admiration, respect, and a quiet envy. Just like our elections. We went, voted, declared our choice for government, and went back to our lives the next day. It's a niceness that's a treasure, one to be cherished, preserved, and handed down to generations to follow. It's a hat we wear, and we wear it so well, the hat of niceness.

Yet, there is a calling; a higher calling; a calling to leadership; a calling to something way higher and greater than what we do now. Somewhere along the line, we have to remove that hat of niceness, not throw it away, not toss it up in the attic, but put it on the most prominent display. Somewhere along the line, we have to take off that hat and put on a real hard hat. It is a hard hat that signifies that we are now ready to lift ourselves from our slumber of niceness and start marching. We have to get ready to put on that real hard hat, and get ready to go into battle. We have to put on that hard hat, or that helmet, and get ready to march out of that tunnel to a thunderous crowd and a roaring applause. We have to put on those helmets and march out through that tunnel to win that big final. We have to start winning the finals, and stop being content with playing the qualifying rounds. We have to go for that gold and stop being content with that great effort that almost got us the bronze. We have to put on that hard hat and aggressively contribute to the world. We can be the front-runners on green technologies. We can be the trailblazer for innovation in technology. We can be the champions that start winning those medals on the first day, and then compete till the very end for the very last ones. We have to wear that hat, that blazing red hat that tells the world that Canada, with its mountains of good will, can do what no other country has done before for world peace, for world justice, and for a new world order. We have to stop being that ancillary unit for the US, be it for technology, trade, oil, or even issues like Afghanistan.

O Canada, let's wake up! With the 30 million that live here, we can be that huge giant that marches with a smile. We're halfway there. During the tough economic times of 2008-2009, we were one of the most resilient economies in the industrialized world and among the G7 nations. Just like our banking system that became a model when the one in our great neighbor down south simply crumbled and led the way into recession. We were one of the last to start facing the effects of the downward spiraling world economy, and one of the first to bounce right out of it. We have it in us.

Wake up to what, you might ask? Wake up and roar, and lead what? Wake up and try, and do what that we are not already doing? We Canadians will be quick to counteract and say this is the way we are. That other way sounds so American, so arrogant, and almost imperialist. When we are a vibrantly alive country, one on the move, one so active, we would become a true bright red North, blazing and alive. We would be a country with a fierce sense of patriotism, a country with a fierce sense of competition, and a country with a fierce sense of being the best in everything. That would be a Canada that steamrolls over any opponent in its path.

It would be that first medal on the first day, the only question being whether it would be Gold, Silver, or Bronze; not when and if that first medal would come. The avenues are endless;

we can be world leaders in aviation, space, information technology, nuclear power, manufacturing, education, and even, my constant reference, sports. A Canada so vibrant and alive would generate wealth so great that we would be able to permanently wipe out our problems of poverty, child poverty and hunger, aging infrastructure, power, all in as little time as one government term.

During one of my first visits back home in 2004, India was well on its path to becoming an economic roaring giant. Along with China, India was blazing its way to one of the fastest growing world economies. The bane that was its vast population suddenly converted into its strength. Any and every business in the world was rushing out to invest, establish itself there, and do business with this growing giant. As I watched TV one day with my father-in-law, Aires, we surfed through a million channels, one of the results of the boom. As we settled down to the Indian edition of an international news channel, the weather segment listed out world temperatures across the globe for the most important international cities; no Canadian city though. The weather was followed by the stock market highlights from around the world, the *NASDAQ*, the *NYSE*, the *DAX*, the *FTSE*, the *NIKKEI* but no *TSX*. "So where is your Canada?" my father-in-law asked me.

I have another bizarre memory from one of my earliest days in Canada. It's a faint memory, but a sure one to this day. I label it as fiction, for want of a good source, but I can't help but write it anyway. It was one of the anniversaries of the US landing on the Moon and, my vague memory tells me, the reference was to the legs of the lunar module that touched down on the Moon. Those legs were apparently made in Canada. I am sure and do hope the headline of that news item I read was half jest, but it said, "We touched down first!" I never could resolve that in my head. But, to this day, it gnaws away at the back of my head. Fiction or true, why do we not have an aggressive space program? Why do we make the legs for the US module as compared with landing our own module on the Moon? When will be the day when the Canadarm will ride a Canadian vehicle to the Moon, to Mars, and beyond? It's a future that's ours to create. It's a tomorrow that we can create. It's a reality that we must create. Many of the lines that precede this may sound nothing short of blatant criticism, or the never happy spirit, or even unpatriotic. It may seem this soul has nothing but criticism for this beautiful and beloved country. Yet, it is only a fierce sense of loyalty and patriotism that generates these thoughts. It's a sense of frustration that lingers when one looks at the potential of this country, this people, and the place that awaits them in world history.

It's a call to a new type of government. It's a call to our politicians, to our leaders, to the business community, to our principals and teachers, doctors, professionals and, most of all, to our youth. It's a call to our sleepy youth; it's a call to wake our kids up to their responsibility and to a better tomorrow.

Can we do it? Do we share something unique as Canadians? Do we believe that together, hand in hand, we can step up to a higher calling? Here is one fascinating example of what is possible. On November 20, 2008, a giant meteorite travelled through Earth's atmosphere, turned into a giant fireball, lit up the sky, and disintegrated into thousands of pieces over the western skies. Thanks to technology, we got it on film; Nature's unplanned majestic show, was captured on those idle parking lot cameras, and many others. As the entire scientific community charged in with glee awaiting the promise of what that held, the search narrowed down to the Alberta-Saskatchewan border. Hundreds of students joined in the search for those thousands of pieces with secrets of the universe hidden in them. It was no ordinary rock that the heavens sent down to us. It was a massive 10-tonne Buzzard Coulee meteorite, named after the Saskatchewan valley where it fell. Even to the naïve and lay mind, the fascination was endless, knowing that this was a rock estimated to be 4.5 billion years old, from somewhere in space, from another world. The value of those pieces? Priceless. However, in real life terms, there is an even more beautiful story that unfolded. While we marveled at the power and beauty of the universe, a very Canadian life story emerged from it all. So, from a story documented by Tarina White in the Edmonton *Sun*, here is a final take on that. It is not just a story about the nobility of mankind, but something uniquely and nobly Canadian.

> CALGARY — Instead of claiming up to $400,000 for the largest known space rock that fell near the Alberta-Saskachewan border last fall, a farmer yesterday donated it to Calgary researchers.
>
> The 13-kilogram rock, roughly the size of a human head, is one of thousands of pieces of a meteorite that exploded in a vibrant fireball in the sky last November before plummeting to Earth.
>
> The largest chunk found so far landed in Alex Mitchell's Saskatchewan field 50 km south of Lloydminster.
>
> A man hunting for pieces of the fallen space rock stumbled across the prize on Mitchell's land and handed it to him as the rightful owner. Inspired by his honesty, Mitchell donated the object he described as "better than gold" to the University of Calgary.
>
> "I won't say we didn't think about the value - it kind of makes your eyes spin," Mitchell said, adding his family kept a few smaller pieces.
>
> "(The man who found the rock) was honest enough to return it to its owner ... and we were an accident that it

was us because it fell on us."

U of C planetary scientist Alan Hildebrand said the black rock is estimated to be 4.5 billion years old.

"There's no way we could afford the kind of money that would be required to buy a specimen of this size," he said.

The 10-tonne Buzzard Coulee meteorite, named after the Saskatchewan valley where the space rock fell on Nov. 20, 2008, fractured into more than 10,000 pieces.

Hundreds of fragments have so far been found, setting the Canadian record for the largest meteorite fall.

TARINA.WHITE@SUNMEDIA.CA

My Canada 207

My Canada

I would like to say, "*My Canada* is a dream that I have" or "*My Canada* is a vision that I have". I don't particularly like the two terms: dream and vision. They represent something lofty, something that requires a lot of effort and personal sacrifice, and a very large movement and struggle, something like the civil liberties movement in the US.

My Canada therefore is a "Simple Dream" that I have. A dream that is real and so doable. *My Canada,* therefore, is a simple vision, the path to which has already been travelled, sadly not all the way for everyone. *My Canada* is a simple reality that requires a simple resolve that says, "Let's do it, now". *My Canada* is a simple yet firm commitment that says, "Let's do it, now". *My Canada* is not a new dream; rather it is an unfulfilled Canadian dream that has not been fulfilled for everyone in this country. *My Canada* is no lofty vision; rather it is a reality that is so seemingly obvious, it is buried right here in plain sight.

I am a dreamer. My wife Lynn is a down to earth realist. She imagines, or simply muses, "Wouldn't it be nice if we…" and I dream away. I say something, which is obviously a stretched dream, and bang…reality comes from her like a bucket full of chilled water. "Not a chance", straight off; no excuses. It's a reality in our married life; it's there in our everyday lives and its there in our every decision. We plan on celebrating her parents' golden jubilee in India and, in a few minutes, my dreams have already travelled to the day, years away, with details of make believe, unending joyous family celebrations. Lynn says, "We could have a new kitchen". She may realistically refer to just a simple new laminated countertop that may cost a few hundred dollars, for which we have already saved up. In my mind, the countertop is already granite, with the rest of the kitchen changed as well, with fancy cabinets and appliances, costing only a few thousands more. I am such a dreamer-realist that I would even have whipped my laptop out, budgeting into the next few months, and salaries, etc.

In a lot of our conversations, Lynn also ends up telling me, "You're shameless", for the way I go about getting things done. I like that compliment. It's a shameless nature, born out of practicality, convenience, and common sense, but above all a spirit of reality. It's a spirit of reality that says, "Why not do it, when it can be done; why not make it happen, when it is possible; and why not succeed, where success is possible?" It's a spirit that says let's get those hands on the tools, figures on paper, and a few nails and planks; later, something will start that will inspire even greater ends. There are lots of events that come to my mind, both fun and serious, that highlight what I am talking about.

When we were very new in Canada, we needed a mattress for Nathan, our elder son. It was a big step, as we moved into our first home and he to his own room for the first time. We needed a twin bed mattress from the store just around the block. It was a two-minute walk and I thought it would take no more than half an hour to have it home. Typical of our world, there was a lot more to it. The saleswoman added a hefty $50 delivery charge for a $250 mattress. I told her that by the time the driver moved to second gear he would be at my place. She would have none of it, and I could not fathom why, after I'd given her my business, she could not make that simple adjustment. Well, I told her, I would carry it home. For a minute, no one said anything, and I saw Lynn take a step back. There I was, the shameless one, getting into my act. The saleswoman, with the greatest smirk, had my mattress brought out and was ready to see the spectacle of a mattress being carried across two very busy intersections. She did manage to stifle her smile and asked how I planned to do it. I told her, in a very matter of fact way, "On my head". I know that by this time Lynn had disowned me and there lay the road to Calvary ahead, all alone. To end a silly story, five minutes later, the mattress was home. I did not pay a penny extra and probably not a single person would have recognized that bloke carrying a mattress. Sure, it turned a few heads, generated a few smiles, created a nice anecdote to share of crazy sights seen, and that's it. For me, that little incident told me that the bridge from where we are to where we want to go, from the Canada of today to the Canada I dream about, is just two signals and a little walk away. It does not need a huge delivery truck, two delivery persons, and a delivery order, and a tip. It needs a simple act, be it a mattress on the head and a walk, or a real concrete action for something that has been staring us in the face for so long. It's doable.

Another time, it was one of my very first winters in Canada. It was still a relatively early time for me, and a driving license and car were still not in the picture. On a particularly bad snowstorm day, I found a colleague in a total state of panic in my office basement parking space. On asking, I got a litany of reasons; the roads were bad; his normal half hour drive would take hours; and, worse, it was time to pick up his two little kids from the day care. "So at least get started", was my automatic reply. "Not so easy", he responded. "My car has broken down and the CAA wait time is almost two hours", he said. It was my first introduction to the CAA. I finally offered to venture out with him to his car to see if we could fix anything. "Let's peek into the engine", I said, asking him to open the hood. "That's not the issue", he said, "It's the tire". By now, I was lost, what did a tire have to do with a broken down car? My dusty, pot holed, and shrapnel littered Indian road memories were by now slowly creeping up on me. "I've got a flat tire", he said. I don't remember my exact reaction; it could have been anything from a hysterical laugh to a shriek of unbelief or just a plain smack in his face. For any Indian and for that matter for any Asian, or African, or Third World nation resident, it is a fact of life. Flat tires happen all the time and you simply replace one with the spare in the boot, and carry on. I've even seen my mom get down on her knees feebly trying to get that jack under the car. It was an easy trick for her, rather than ask for help. The sight of that was enough to get enough men scampering over to help. The end of that story…it took us 15 minutes to get that flat tire changed. It was a weird learning experience — to know that someone could come to change your tire, or to know that a flat tire could be the end of the world for somebody. I did sign up for CAA, first thing, when I bought my first car, a 10-year-old van, actually, but then it was more to do with the age of that van, and not to enjoy the luxury of someone changing my flat tire.

It's a shameless nature and spirit that tells me to roll up my sleeves and get down on my knees and change the tire. A simple cardboard on the floor takes care of my pants, and those tools lying idly in the boot and a little physical activity stretching those muscles and there it's done. It's a spirit that drives me nuts, because it makes me see things that are doable, where people say no. It's a spirit that tells me to go the extra step and shake a hand, give a hug, and don't feel bad to say sorry. It's a spirit that is common everywhere, born out of humanity. Remember how you did not hesitate to put your bag down and help that lady haul that walker up the bus? Never mind that the front wheels of the walker were covered with dirty slushy snow; never mind the fact that the walker was loaded with grocery bags, baby bags and, of course, the baby too. Remember how good you felt? You were definitely not ashamed as you dusted your hands, picked up your bag, and crammed yourself after the lady into the crowded bus.

Does your child have a scooter, one of those ultra modern, super fast, all shiny metal, *Razor* scooter? They all do, and they love to zoom around on it, round the block. They also get tired pretty fast, and they also discover pretty soon, that you can ride it quite fast yourself. If you passed by my street, a few summers back, while the kids were still little, and if in an instant you saw Lynn disappear from the porch, well one reason could be that I was up to something silly. So, if I can lay claim to being the first scooter-dad, I would happily put Ethan standing in the front part of that little footrest of the scooter, wedge in a foot, and like a giant polar bear on a little scooter, zoom away up and down the street with Ethan having the best ride ever. Hey, what did I care; Ethan got a super fast free ride; I got a fun ride, too; and then I knew I had done something special and spent some real quality time with my son! It's that spirit I am talking about. It's that spirit that is needed in every one who has, and who can do it for those who do not.

It's that spirit that tells those CEOs with millions in bonuses that there is a lot more they can do, over and above a few counted charity dollars calculated against a tax break. One of our biggest mistakes is to count the dollars and leave out the person. What if every CEO, every academic, every scientist, every accountant, every teacher, and every citizen, took out an hour a month, and did something that they had never done before? Ride a scooter with those few who needed that special talent that only they could provide. Remember Sir Conrad Black, the Canadian-born British gentleman, publishing magnate, historian and so many other great things? Well, for whatever reason, he ended up in the Colman federal correctional complex to serve a six-and-a-half-year sentence. He also turned out to be one of the most popular inmates. What did Sir Conrad do to merit such a standing? He taught French, piano, American history, and even personal history. Were they boring classes? They were the most sought after classes, with his personal history ones being the most amusing ones. It even invited offers from US and Canadian publishing houses for his lectures to be published. To top it all off, seeing the small-time drug dealer, the Puerto Rican fisherman, the *Sopranos*-like New York *Mafia* bill collector, and a colourful variety of such individuals, graduate under his teaching. However, the greatest achievement of them all, teaching inmates to write books.

The summer of 2008 was such a one for me as I heard the announcements, at the end of Sunday Mass, asking for volunteers to teach and prepare kids for their Confirmation. For a Catholic, it is a major sacrament and equivalent to passing into religious adulthood. I ignored that request, for a few Sundays, till the repeated announcements slowly began to play on my conscience. I had taught before, decades ago, and those were little kids. Here was a request to teach teenagers, Canadian teenagers, actually grade eight kids. I had seen them everywhere, on the buses, in the malls, and all those places they hang out, pretending to be adults. The thought was scary, and Lynn encouraged me with the warning, "It's teens, you better do well". I finally did volunteer and teach during that fall and winter. It turned out to be one of the most amazing experiences of my life. They were little adults alright, but not the kind I had seen in the malls. These were the same teens, with faith like a rock, unbelievable conviction, and a drive that would make a politician squirm. It opened a whole new chapter in my life, knowing the power and promise that exists in the little unexplored worlds of these youth. In my very first class, I teased them with the question, "If there were no parents, no priests, and no school involved in this, if it was totally your choice, would you be here?" The force and the blast of the one-voiced equivocal "Yes" did wonders for me. As the influential *Maclean*'s magazine in its April 2009 issue around the same time said:

> *For the first time in ages, fewer teens are drinking, using drugs and having sex. What's going on...a generation that tends to examine its own urges on a meta-level, accommodating and managing them in ways older people could scarcely imagine*[20].

If every accountant in this country taught for just a few hours a year, taught anyone who could learn that skill and add it to a resume; those few hours would help a kid to move from selling burgers to gain that little extra confidence and go on to an accounting career. It would help an immigrant accountant gain that little extra edge to break through on a much-needed job. Those pearls of wisdom that could only be had from the mouths of the experienced ones would make all the difference between breaking through that unemployment jinx or falling back into depression and social security. That one free class would make the difference between having just enough and poverty. If every Bay street investor took a few hours a year and taught; taught those who needed it how to convert those few hundred hard-earned dollars into thousands; those words of wisdom would help make a first time investor's puny little thousand into a lifetime secure investment. It would make a hundred new millionaires.

If every geek in this country took time, and their own laptop and, in millions of classrooms across the country, taught little kids, big kids, the computer illiterate, the seniors; what a difference it would make to those millions, given that we stand in an IT era and those precious few shortcuts and tricks made the difference between a school dropout and a future Bill Gates!

If every specialist doctor took a few hours a year to visit those far away from the big hospitals in the cities, and bring them relief from something that would have meant a diagnosis too late.

If our big oil companies, the famous vilified ones, the big banks, the Credit Card companies, and corporations, took a tiny percent of their billions in profits and invested it back in our students, sportsmen, environment, and society; it would make a huge difference between a society that exists and a society that excels. During the 2008 federal elections, a simple 45 million dollar grant taken away from the arts was one of the culprits that cost a government a potential majority. That same year, with a booming oil market, the energy and resources sector made billions in profit. What would a tiny fraction of that, something equivalent to a tiny 45 million dollars, do? Today, we lack sufficient government funding in almost every sphere of life, and we cry and complain about it. Yet, in the type of society we live, the disparities between the haves and have-nots are so huge.

Do we need to scare ourselves of something called socialism when we talk of providing for those who have not? No, rather a simple religion called humanity, a little thought called caring, and a little helping hand called sharing, can work miracles in so many areas of our society. As passionate as we are about human rights around the world, we tend to forget about them when it comes our own have nots. We can hide behind ideologies, or preach them. We can let them scare us, or let them encourage us. We could label it socialism, or we could declare ourselves fiscal conservatives. We could believe in lots more taxes, or in slashing of taxes. But, in the end, what matters is what reaches out and lifts up the ones that may languish for years, or even generations. We are, all, good at heart and mean well, but the *when*, that is what matters. Our policies implemented now may help the generations to come, but we need to actively think of the ones that need help now.

That is the Canada I dream of, the Canada where we take time to dump our big selves on those little scooters and give someone a ride. We are a country that connects, connects in so many ways; yet, somewhere, even though we may not admit it, we lose the reality or the effectiveness of that connection. It's those little communities, those little acts of connection that could make the difference. We could go from week to week, Sunday to Sunday, happily nestled in our little comfy caves and not realize that all around us, in those same neighbourhoods, a few minutes out there could bring to life a new country.

It would be a new Canada that says more in a nod than just a mere cursory acknowledgement of a stranger. A nod from that CEO to that paint-splattered workman he meets on his way acknowledging a student from a weekend class, and a thank you, have a nice day, a new week, till the next time when we are teacher and student again. A nod from that big time investor to a janitor in those overalls that says, "Don't worry, follow that advice and your hundred dollars is safe". A nod that says, "Next time we meet, we'll see how to turn that hundred into a thousand". Hundreds of nods that tell the country, that tells Canadians, that we are connecting. Hundreds of nods saying that for every single Canadian that is lifted out of poverty, for every single Canadian that succeeds, this country is better for it; that for every single Canadian that is lifted out of social support, there is one more

Canadian living decently, and contributing to society; that for every child that gets breakfast, every single day, a future successful citizen is formed.

What if that single hour on a Sunday afternoon became the Canadian hour? What if that single hour on a Sunday afternoon became the reactor for a country on the move? What if that single hour on a Sunday afternoon became a happy hour for every Canadian to give and to receive? What if that single hour on a Sunday afternoon saw every Canadian out somewhere, out of their little nests, and looking to add another twig to a broken nest?

It's a Canadian spirit that would make a rich divided country into super rich united one. It's a Canadian spirit that would make a country, now divided by poverty, united as one that has no poor. It's a Canadian sprit that would make this country a shining beacon, for which no award was ever invented.

How much would it take to get 30 million citizens out on to the streets in a country where there are not enough people to fill every sidewalk? And, then, in those millions of hands held together to form the largest chain ever, will we find a Canada that is waiting to be discovered.

So, what happened to that anniversary celebration in India or that new counter top in our kitchen? They both did happen, a lot more differently from the first imaginative dream. A lot of planning, moving around a few dollars, some sacrifices, a lot of phone calls, quotes and some persuasive pushing and they happened. As Canadians, with all our means and resources, we can make it happen. As Canadians, with a spirit that naturally reaches out to that kid fallen off his bike on the street, or to that senior struggling up the steps, or to that Canadian struggling hard to partake of the goodness that everyone else is enjoying, we can make it happen.

It's that same spirit of reality that tells me, let's imagine the pros and cons when we sit back for our first break; for now, let's just do it. I like the term so prevalent in IT, "proof of concept"; in real life, it could mean the first university class for someone who never imagined it. Ever so often, we believe we can change a situation; be the first to fix it; so let's not allow somebody else to get a bruised toe on the same rock sticking out of the ground. And, then, maybe later, we say, and give ourselves enough time to imagine a thousand cons and deal with them. When it involves people's lives, our kids future, and a tomorrow that can be lost forever, then it's that same spirit that says, "Let's just do it".

Brighter Red: A New Tomorrow

Brighter Red: A New Tomorrow

So, what is the Canada of tomorrow?

Do you see it? Do you see it in your success, professional and personal? Do you see it in the big RRSP payment coupled with all those returns that you will reap from your investments? Do you see your success in being called a snowbird, a comfortably retired Canadian, who can fly away at will from the snow and be back for the summer, with not a care in the world? Do you see your success in creating that large corporation and passing it on to your children?

We have to be ready to take a leap. We have to be ready to envision something so radically new that the current good seems obsolete. We have to be ready to take a bold step forward that would ask us to first stop, bend backwards, bend low, rather uncomfortably, help lift up those who have not made it, and then carry on. We have to be ready to make that red on our Maple Leaf, truly a blaze, and a beacon of hope for every single one of us called Canadians.

And, then, looking out at the world, we have to be ready to challenge the notion that we as Canadians are happy to follow, most of the time. We have to be ready to challenge our role, set policies, and lead the world in new directions. We have to be ready to challenge our neighbours as leaders of the free world. We have to be ready to stop living in the shadow of the others that dominate the news and set the path to tomorrow. We have to be willing to look in and see that among the 30 million that live here, there are champions, leaders, visionaries, and maybe revolutionaries even. We have to be ready to start winning those medals in every sport from day one. We have to be ready to show the world that we cannot just educate, rather we can create the best. We have to be ready to tell the world that we can lead, lead the world to a greener planet, lead the world in eliminating hunger, eliminating poverty, eliminating suffering. We have to show the world that we don't just provide for all, but rather we provide for all in abundance.

We have to be, first and foremost, willing to tell ourselves that something is not so well with our sense of comfort, our sense of complacency, our sense of niceness, our sense of goodness and, most of all, our sense of having done it all. We have to be willing to take a step, first to the side, and see that all is not well. We have to be willing to take a step backwards and start reinvesting in the lost, the havenots and in those that society and life have left behind? And then, we have to be willing to tell ourselves, that this land, this huge free land, blessed with an abundance of wealth in every form, can provide in plenty for all Canadians. It is a challenge for us to rise way beyond the status quo. For, to us that have received so much, there is also the challenge of rising that much higher.

Somewhere along the way, as we join forces, politicians, academics, scientists, sports men and women, youth, seniors, veterans, the day to day workers, the ones on the buses and trains, the men and women who decide policy and the ones who implement policy, the business men and women that create the wealth, and the men and women who work to make it happen, the women that rock the cradle at home, and the women who operate the fork lifts, the women who stand in front and teach, and the women who mother us through our infancy, the women that lead and the women that create the leaders, we are all such a huge force.

A vibrant new Canada that can move from being a slumbering beast to being a roaring rampaging lion. It is doable. A vibrant new Canada that can conquer itself and the ills of this world. It is doable. A vibrant new Canada that can go from being a passing mention to the front page. That is a Canada that is doable; that is a Canada that I envision; that is a Canada that I dream of; that is a Canada I hope to inspire; that is a Canada that, I hope, wakes up and sees itself. That is a Canada that I dream is oh so possible, yet not so far away. That is a Canada that cares not just for its own, but has enough to help others, too.

A Canada that is doable, not in the next decade, but a Canada that is doable **now**. A Canada that sets aside all its distractions and decides that now is the time, now is the moment that we'll refer to in future as the moment it changed — Canada changed. The moment when the red on that proud Canadian maple leaf became a truly *Brighter Red*.

References

i   Laurie, Nathan. " THE COST OF POVERTY" An analysis of the economic cost of poverty in Ontario; OAFB, November 2008; Page 4; http://www.oafb.ca/assets/pdfs/CostofPoverty.pdf

ii   "Breaking the cycle of Poverty". Ontario's Poverty Reduction Strategy; http://www.children.gov.on.ca/htdocs/English/growingstronger/index.aspx

iii   Ibid

iv   Ibid

v   "Down, out and hidden away in Oakville"; Saturday, January 2, 2010 Toronto Edition; thestar.com; http://www.thestar.com/article/510759

vi   Greg deGroot-Maggetti. "A measure of poverty in Canada" A guide to the debate about poverty lines; March 2002; http://action.web.ca/home/cpj/attach/A_measure_of_poverty.pdf

vii   Ibid

viii   Scott, Andy. "A salute to Phil Fontaine"; Published Friday June 12th, 2009

ix   Ibid.

x   Ibid.

xi   Brown, Louise. "Cash payments encourage college students to stay the course"; April 29, 2009; http://www.collegesontario.org/news/colleges-in-the-news/cash-payments-encourage-college-students-to-stay-the-course.html

xii   Breaking the Cycle of Poverty". Ontario's Poverty Reduction Strategy; http://www.children.gov.on.ca/htdocs/English/growingstronger/index.aspx

xiii   "Roots of Youth Violence". November 2008; http://www.rootsofyouthviolence.on.ca/english/reports.asp

xiv   Annual Report on Ontario's School 2008." People for Education; http://www.peopleforeducation.com/reportonschools08

xv   Rately, John J. "Can exercise help people learn?; "http://johnratey.typepad.com/

xvi   "Building a Green Economic Stimulus Package for Canada". 2009; http://www.sustainableprosperity.ca/files/Building%20a%2Green%20Economic%20Stimulus%20Package%20for%20Canada.pdf

xvii   Chippewas of Nawash First Nation. "Comments on Ontario Hydro's ''Comprehensive'' Study"; November 1998; http://www.ccnr.org/nawash.html

xviii   Legislative Assembly of Ontario; http://www.ontla.on.ca/web/home.do

xix   Elections Canada On-line; http://www.elections.ca/content_youth.asp?section=yth&dir=bas/faq&document=index&lang=e#q15

xx   Gillis, Charlie, Macleans.ca. "Generation tame". April 13, 2009; Pages 36-40; http://www2.macleans.ca/2009/04/10/generation-tame/

Index

A

anecdotes
  2008 federal election,
    campaigning 171
  alaska, anchorage airport 14
  first nations, write a chapter on 78
  golf, indoor 135
  Jay, coffee, bums 58
  lunch, Mother Teresa, 6 yr old 43
  mattress, delivery 210
  McDonalds, shoot, Harper 176
  poor, downtown, loonie 58
  Queen Street, mistaken
    minister 188
  scooter-dad 213
  Shurta, driving test, Oman, 174
  snowstorm, flat-tire, CAA 211
  TDSB, Christmas gift 163
  TDSB, first winter, first flurries 163
  Toronto Star, vending machine 158
  TSX 203
  volunteer, teach confirmation 214
  X-files, Canada 30

B

Banks
  Canadian banking system,
    model 202
  Brighter Red 225

C

canada, canadians
  Adams, Bryan, summer of 69 31
  barbarians, Iran, execution,
    abortion 160
  Black, Sir Conrad, Publishing
    magnate, historian, inmate,
    popular 214
  Buzzard Coulee, meteorite,
    Saskatchewan, U of C 205, 206
  Charter of Rights and
    Freedoms 173
  Chrétien, Jean Aline 170
  PM 170
  Stockwell Day, opposition
    leader 170
  discrimination, racial 15, 57
  fierce sense of best in
    everything 202
  competition 202
  patriotism 202
  haves, have-nots 22, 216
  Highway of Heroes 20
  human rights, civil rights 160
  immigrant's journey 36
  Mulroney, Brian 35
  of the, evolution theme,
    creation theme 173
  Our Father, classrooms, weaned 171
  politically correct 159
  religion of secularism 159
  religious diversity,
    Merry Christmas 159, 163
  religious wishes Eid Mubarak,
    Happy Hanukak 159
  Happy Christmas 166
  Russell Peters
  Indian accent 164
  Mumbai stench 81
  world cup, world event 197
  secret hidden agenda 173
  tent cities 192
  Trudeau, Pierre 35

D

democracy
coalition Dion, Stéphane 176
Duceppe, Gilles 176
Harper, Stephen 176
Layton, Jack 176
united opposition 190
cost of leader's security 191
disguise, kings, generals 187
diversity, thought, opinion, agenda 176
Han dynasty, prince, common people, XunZi 189
Harper, Stephen blue-ribbon panel 179
election, 2008, budget 189
no confidence votes 178
Hazelton, B.C., deprivation, tragedy, and suicide 186
Ignatieff, Michael blue-ribbon panel 179
election threat, EI 190
first declaration 178
Legislative Assembly, role of MPP 184
Martin, Paul deficits 170
sponsorship scandal 185
McGuinty, Dalton, Premier, education funding 189
negative campaigning conservative war machine 177
liberal hypocrisy 177
question period 71, 177
CBC panel, description 177
security, leaders, wall 188
Wynne, Kathleen, minister of education, ontario 188

E

education
1800, British North America, King Edward VII 102
Breaking the cycle of poverty 99
cash incentives for at risk students 93
human capital 97
Indian Institute of Technology 101
OISE 93, 98, 100
paper on a Proposed New Model 104
poverty children, higher risk 99
Federal Canadian University 105
high poverty students 100
publicly funded, education, India 94
racial/ethnic minority gap, achievement 99
RESP 94
theory of essentialism 100
theory of individualism 100
tuition 101
tuition fee 94
University of Toronto, insulin 101
vicious cycle of poverty 96

F

first nations
Archbishop Desmond Tutu 78, 80, 85
boiling water advisories 81
Chief Phil Fontaine 79, 85, 86, 89
Government of Canada apology 79
Indian Residential Schools Settlement 79
Pope Benedict XVI, sorrow 79
Dances with Wolves, Kevin Costner 77
DART team 82
E Coli 82, 86, 88
H1N1 rapid spread 83
sanitizer, alcohol-abuse, 87
health related issues HIV, Aids, suicide, birth defects, infant mortality 85
Human Rights report destitution, deprivation, and dependency 80
Kashechewan reserve 88
Kelowna Agreement 86
mass evacuation 82
Michaëlle Jean Governor General, seal heart, university in the Arctic North 88
mould-infested homes 88
National Aboriginal Day 79
over crowding house fire deaths, five-year-old Tristan Mousseau, nine-year-old Hope Richard 83
Scott, Andy 80, 85
A salute to Phil Fontaine, June 2009 79
skin diseases scabies, impetigo, rash covered bodies 82

INDEX

Third World 75, 77, 80, 81, 82, 85

G

green
  Al Gore, Nobel Prize 144
  Chippewas of Nawash, people, earth, interconnected 152
  Dion, Stéphane, carbon tax 144
  global warming 143, 146, 147
  Green Economic Stimulus Package 151
  Green Party 145
  hybrid cars 149
  Kyoto Accord 143
  misconception, conservative, republican 145
  nuclear energy 142, 143, 147, 148, 151, 203
  President Obama, cap-and-trade 145
  Scylla, Prison break 141
  slogan, TCDSB 144
  Venus, planet, runaway greenhouse effect 146

H

health care
  educated, healthier workforce 97
  for every kind of ailment 44
  politician's responsibility 174
  poverty, mental, physical issues 51
USA envy 52

I

India
  Congress Party 170
  election cartoons 185
  fastest growing world economies 203
  large democracy, MPs 178
  leaders, religious holidays, wishes 161
  Motherland, Mother India 21
  political conventions and rallies 171
  religious diversity Diwali, Dussera 161, 162
  Eid, Ramadan 161, 162
  religions-Hindus, Muslims, Sikhs, Buddhists, Jains, Catholics, Christians, Jews 160
  sports 132
  tray of sweets 162

M

My Canada
  a simple dream, reality, resolve, vision, firm commitment 209
  Bill Gates 216
  Canadarm 204
  Humanity in Canada 60
  Jesus Christ, Christmas 159
  mountains of good will 202
  MP, MPP commoner 184
  in the riding 186, 193
  jobs, investment 186
  social activities 185

N

nations
  Afghanistan 201, 202
  Australia 132
  Bangkok 14
  Bangladesh 169
  Belarus 169
  Brazil 169
  China 127, 132, 169, 189, 203
  Cuba 127
  Germany 22
  Hong Kong 13, 14
  Indonesia 169
  Iran 169
  Iraq 169
  Italy 169
  Jamaica 169
  Middle East 13, 27, 29, 35, 36, 174, 175, 197, 198
  New Zealand 31
  Oman, Muscat 14, 27, 30, 31
  Pakistan 169
  Peru 169
  Philippines 169
  Portugal 169
  Sri Lanka 169
  Ukraine 169
  Zimbabwe 127

O

O Canada
  Canada-Day 20
  Huynh, Carol, gold medal, podium 129
  national anthem, inspiring, emotion 41

P

poverty
  Breaking the Cycle Ontario's poverty reduction strategy, children living in poverty 54
  child soldiers, child workers, hungry children 73
  Citizens for Public Justice, paper, Greg deGroot-Maggetti, children, meaning of poverty 71
  Food Bank 53, 71
  Habitat for Humanity, Food or Shelter, ad 41
  health issues, poor, physical and mental ailments 51
  India, children begging 70
  Jamie Oliver, Tony Blair, food in schools 68
  Make Poverty History 54
  Malaise, Wikipedia, definition 51
  Mother Teresa's ashrams, for the destitute 43
  newspaper headlines, online 51
  Ontario Association of Food Banks report, GDP, cost of poverty 53
  Phan Th Kim Phúc, suffering, children 65
  Poor Canadians 52
  program, Out of the Cold 58
  Revenue Canada, definition of poverty, consumption basket, equity-based, mixed consumption and equity-based measures 59
  The Grocery Foundation, ad, hungry school children 66

R

recession
  banks 202
  Canada, job losses 97
  consensus budget 190
  creating jobs 172
  elections 178
  financially hurting citizens 190
  G20 summit 68
  GM and Chrysler 60
  government aid, billions 60
  hurting nation 190
  opposition parties funding 190
  partisanship 190
  US $700 billion stimulus plan 190
  US, job losses 189
  warranties of new cars 60

S

sports
  Active Healthy Kids Canada 127
  Beijing Summer Olympics 126
  Blue Jays, Rogers Centre 134
  Chuck e Cheese's, McDonald's or Wendy's 128
  Citius, Altius, Fortius Faster, Higher, Stronger 128
  Huynh, Carol first gold, Bejing Olympics 129
  Hazelton, B.C 129
  Sullivan, Joe, Coach 130, 131, 135
  United Church congregation 130
  Vietnamese immigrants, boat people 129
  Igali, Daniel, Sydney Olympics, wrestler, Nigeria, Canadian flag 131
  March Break, inactive kids 128
  monetary reward, olympics, Harper Government 133
  People for Education\ Annual Report on Ontario's School 2008 127
  physical education teacher 127
  Rately, Dr. John J, physical activity, brain 127
  Reed, Gary, olympics, medals, poverty 132
  school sports Day, India, school, high jump, long jump, triple jump, discuss, shot put, javelin, 136
  Sony PS3s, XBox 360s, Wiis 127
  Statistics Canada 126
  Sundin, Matt 132

INDEX

Trupish, Adam, boxer, 2008 olympics, personal debt 137

T

taxes
 auto industry bailout 60
 carbon tax 145
 child poverty, additional revenue 55
 cost of education 96
 Dalton McGuinty, Health tax, HST 146
 income tax 146
 Oman, no tax 27
 property tax 146
 tax rebate on hybrid cars 149
 T-word 30

U

USA
 Canada Health Care, envy 52
 civil liberties movement 209
 first visit, blunt, arrogant, rude 165
 H-1B, green card 30
 Obama, African-American president 199
 superpower, only one 198

V

violence and crime
 Acts
 2007 Youth Criminal Justice Act 117
 black youth Jackson, Rev Jesse 118
 NBA stars, Raptors 118
 Smith, Will 118
 Creba, Jane, 15-yr old, shot, boxing day 115, 116
 Jordan Manners, 15-yr old, shot, school 113
 Melton, Frank, Mayor Mississippi 118
 Roots of Youth Violence, report, 2008 113
 St. Remy Jarvis, shot, 18-yr old, bus stop 115
 Clemee Joseph, mother 115

W

world leaders
 Blair, Tony, kids meals 68
 Bush, George, end of term 199
 Gandhi, Mahatma 42
 Mandela, Nelson 42
 Reagan, Ronald, government, problem 172
 Sarkozy, Nicholas, middle east peace efforts 198

Y

youth
 2008 US election 199
 canadian, elections, one spark 200
 Catholic Schools United Nations Assembly 200
 Maclean's, April 2009 issue, Canadian teens, drinking, drugs, sex 215

About the Author

Arriving in Canada in 1999 as a new immigrant, it was an instant love with his new adopted country. Starting life with a young family from the real basics helped him quickly gauge the struggles and challenges faced by new immigrants as well as those at the lowest strata of Canadian society.

This is Kevin Lobo's first book and it arises from a passion to see the Canadian dream fulfilled to full measure for every single Canadian.

When not writing about the social realities around him or administering SQL Server databases, Kevin spends his time helping at his local Church, teaching youth in the parish, being the home handyman, and volunteering for other social causes.